The Irish Civil War

and what it still means for the Irish people

by Frances M. Blake

Information on Ireland

First published in 1986 by Information on Ireland, PO Box 958,
London W14 0JF

Copyright © Frances M. Blake, 1986

Designed by Pat Kahn
Typeset and printed by The Russell Press Ltd., Gamble Street,
Nottingham NG7 4ET

ISBN 0 9507381 8 2

Trade distribution by Turnaround Distribution, 27 Horsell Road,
London N5 1XL, tel. 01-609 7836

*Front cover photograph: Michael Collins leading the pro-treaty army at
the state funeral of Arthur Griffith in August 1922.*

*Title page: a Free State soldier prepares to fire on the Hamman Hotel,
Dublin, which became the Republican headquarters after the fall of the
Four Courts.*

*Opposite: a patrol of the IRA's Third Western Division in Sligo, May
1922.*

British Library Cataloguing in Publication Data
Blake, Frances M.
    The Irish civil war 1922-1923 and what it still means for the Irish people.
    1. Ireland — History — Civil War, 1922-1923
    2. Ireland — Politics and government — 1922-1949
    I. Title   II. Information on Ireland
    941.5082'2   DA963
    ISBN 0-9507381-8-2

About the author

Frances M. Blake was born and educated in England. In the mid-1970s she sorted and catalogued one of the largest collections of historical documents of the civil war period for the archives department of University College Dublin. Following her work on the papers of Republican officer Ernie O'Malley, she compiled and edited his best-selling book on the civil war, *The Singing Flame*.

Information on Ireland

Information on Ireland is a voluntary group which publishes information about the situation in Ireland that is of concern to people in Britain but is not available through the national media. Formed in 1978, the group is independent and non-profit-making.

If you would like a list of our publications, send a stamped addressed envelope to: Information on Ireland, PO Box 958, London W14 0JF.

Donations to help us in our work are very welcome. Please make cheques/POs payable to Information on Ireland.

Inset: James Connolly. Main picture: the Irish Citizen Army on parade outside Liberty Hall, the Irish Transport and General Workers' Union headquarters.

'If you remove the English army tomorrow and hoist the green flag over Dublin Castle, unless you set about the organization of the Socialist Republic your efforts would be in vain.

'England would still rule you. She would rule you through her capitalists, through her landlords, through her financiers, through the whole array of commercial and individualist institutions she has planted in this country'.

James Connolly, 1897

'It is felt that the proposal [for the partition of Ireland] to leave the Home Rule minority at the mercy of an ignorant majority with the evil record of the Orange party is a proposal that should never have been made, and that the establishment of such a scheme should be resisted with armed force if necessary.

'Personally I entirely agree with those who think so; Belfast is bad enough as it is; what it would be under such rule the wildest imagination cannot conceive... the Orangemen would have scant regards for the rights of the minority left at their mercy.

'Such a scheme would destroy the Labour movement by disrupting it. It would perpetuate in a form aggravated in evil the discords now prevalent, and help the Home Rule and Orange capitalists and clerics to keep their rallying cries before the public as the political watchwords of the day.'

James Connolly, March 1914

Donegal

Derry

ULSTER

Antrim

Tyrone

NORTHERN IRELAND

Down

Fermanagh

Armagh

Monaghan

Sligo

Mayo

Leitrim

Cavan

Louth

Roscommon

CONNACHT

Longford

Meath

Galway

Westmeath

Kildare

Dublin

Offaly

LEINSTER

Wicklow

Laois

Clare

Kilkenny

Carlow

Tipperary

Limerick

MUNSTER

Wexford

Waterford

Kerry

Cork

Introduction

At the start of the twentieth century the island of Ireland was still one country of 32 counties, although not a free and independent nation. It had been wholly integrated into the United Kingdom despite a long history of resistance to British rule. Since the dissolution in 1800 of the brief home-ruled parliament in Dublin, accomplished by massive bribes and corruption, there had always been Irish MPs sitting in the House of Commons, and all Ireland was governed directly from Westminster.

However, the spirit of rebellion, existing ever since the first conquest in 1172, was kept alive throughout the nineteenth century so that by 1912 successive British governments had come to realise that some restoration of home rule was necessary in the hope of thwarting more militant resistance.

The Home Rule Bill for Ireland was never enacted. Britain willingly capitulated to threats from the Unionists in Ulster (those who were mostly the plantation stock of the sixteenth and seventeenth centuries) especially when senior British army officers openly supported them. Then the outbreak of the First World War allowed Britain the excuse to put aside the rights of the Irish people as a whole. Two years later came one of the most historic events in Ireland's history.

It was the Irish Republican Brotherhood (IRB), inheritors of the Fenian armed force tradition, who planned the 1916 Easter Rising in Dublin, acting on the principle that 'England's difficulty is Ireland's opportunity'. Several strands of nationalism were involved, including the clearly defined socialism of James Connolly and the more romantic but also clear-headed idealism of Patrick Pearse. All these were opposed to John Redmond's Irish MPs at Westminster, who had in their turn inherited the prototype constitutional nationalist position of Daniel O'Connell. Like O'Connell a century before, the Redmondites attempted and failed to achieve Irish freedom by means of the British parliamentary system.

There was no country-wide insurrection in 1916 and in British circles the Rising was seen as a failure. It was followed by court-martial executions of the Irish leaders. The establishment of the time made much of the Dublin public's displayed hostility to the Rising, as well as counting on mass condemnations from press, politicians and church. It was a mistaken impression. As was to be seen again and again up to the present time, whenever Irish republicans are killed and persecuted by the *British* in Ireland, the results have a powerful influence on the consciousness of the Irish people, drawing on collective memories of 800 years of invasion.

The last general election held for Britain and all of Ireland took place in 1918, and the Irish party, Sinn Fein, won a decisive majority of seats in their own island. Sinn Fein had been founded in 1905 by Arthur Griffith. He was conservative on social and economic issues and supported the idea of a dual monarchy for Britain and Ireland but with separate parliaments in London and Dublin. However, most of those imprisoned after the 1916 Rising were released within a year and their presence strengthened the incoming republican elements within Sinn Fein. Eamon de Valera became the party's president, being a leading survivor of 1916, but Griffith retained power by accepting the vice-presidential post.

Right: a recruiting leaflet for the Irish Citizen Army in 1913. The great Dublin lock-out strike was one reason for its formation.

Below: the Connaught Rangers were an Irish regiment in the British army who mutinied in India in 1920 in protest at atrocities committed by the Black and Tans in Ireland. On the left is part of the Times *report of 5 July 1920. On the right is a photo of Private James Joseph Daly who was executed by firing squad.*

TAMPERING WITH THE ARMY.

SINN FEIN IN INDIA.

CONNAUGHT RANGERS MUTINY.

(FROM OUR OWN CORRESPONDENT.)

SIMLA (received yesterday).

A number of men of the Connaught Rangers have refused to do duty on the ground of the alleged wrongs inflicted on Ireland. The situation is, happily, well in hand, and only a section of the regiment is affected. The trouble began at Jullundur (Punjab), where half a battalion is stationed, forming the British garrison.

The men involved represented to the commanding officer that they were no longer able to serve, but that they were quite prepared to draw their pay. They appear to have been respectful, and intimated their willingness to give up their arms to any British troops sent to relieve them. They have since been disarmed and over 200 are under guard. The Seaforths and the Welch Regiment are now at Jullundur.

REASONS WHY

YOU SHOULD JOIN

The Irish Citizen Army.

BECAUSE It pledges its members to work for, organise for, drill for and fight for **an Independent Ireland.**

BECAUSE It places its reliance upon the only class that never betrayed Ireland—the Irish Working Class.

BECAUSE Having a definite aim to work for there is no fear of it being paralysed in the moment of action by divisions in its Executive Body.

BECAUSE It teaches that "the sole right of ownership of Ireland is vested in the people of Ireland, and that that full right of ownership may, and ought to be, enforced by any and all means that God hath put within the power of man."

BECAUSE It works in harmony with the Labour and true National Movements and thus embraces all that makes for Social Welfare and National Dignity.

Companies Wanted in Every District.

RECRUITS WANTED EVERY HOUR.

Apply for further information, Secretary, Citizen Army, Liberty Hall, Dublin.

Irish Paper.]   *City Printing Works, 13 Stafford Street, Dublin.*

Sinn Fein's successful candidates met and set up the first Dail Eireann (the Irish people's own national assembly) to organise their own national administration. Although soon declared illegal by a British decree, the Dail continued to function even when forced underground and with many of its democratically elected representatives imprisoned.

More ominous than these political developments for the British was the existence of Sinn Fein's military partner, the Irish Republican Army, which fought an increasingly successful guerrilla war against them from 1919-21, despite very powerful odds. At Easter 1916 two republican militant forces had joined together as the army of the Irish Republic: no longer the Irish Volunteers or the Irish Citizen Army but one army of the Republic. The forms of struggle pioneered in Ireland were adopted in India, Egypt, Palestine, Cyprus, Kenya and elsewhere. It was the first colonial conflict to seriously undermine the British imperial system although it was incomplete. At the time, Lenin at once recognised the significance of Irish nationalism as a revolutionary force.

That significance was also very apparent to the British ruling class and they urgently needed a solution on their own terms. Their first move was in 1920 during the height of what were euphemistically called 'the troubles' in Ireland. The British parliament, which would not enact Home Rule, passed instead the Government of Ireland Act. This legislation arranged for two separate parliaments in Ireland, one for *six* of Ulster's *nine* counties (in a gerrymandering operation *par excellence*), and one for the remaining twenty-six. The plan was, of course, for both 'Northern' and 'Southern' states to remain under British sovereignty in the classic method of divide and rule.

The six-counties election was held in May 1921, resulting in an inevitable Unionist victory when they won 40 seats to six each for Sinn Fein and the old Nationalist (constitutionalist) party. The Unionist leader, Sir James Craig, was sworn in as prime minister and the following month King George V came to Belfast to open the Stormont parliament and grant it devolved powers, including the vital responsibility for law and order. A wave of killings, reprisals and riots followed, and has been periodically repeated ever since.

From 1919-21 the IRA's battle with the British crown forces intensified. The IRA's courage and determination, aided by growing popular support, forced the British to parley with Irish politicians and to seek to gain at the conference table what they were unable to win in the field.

Oʒlaiʒ na h-Éireann.

Áṁ-Oifiʒ, áṫ Cliaṫ.   General Headquarters, Dublin

Department..............
Reference No..............

9th. July, 1921.

TO:
Officers Commanding All Units.

In view of the conversations now being entered
into by our Government with the Government of Great
Britain, and in pursuance of mutual understandings
to suspend hostilities during these conversations,
active operations by our troops will be suspended
as from Noon Monday July. Eleventh.

C/S.

*The official announcement of the July 1921 truce by the
IRA's GHQ.*

A truce

On 9 July 1921 the following communiqué from General Headquarters in
Dublin was sent to all IRA units, signed by Richard Mulcahy, the Chief of
Staff:

> In view of the conversations now being entered into by our Government
> with the Government of Great Britain, and in pursuance of mutual

conversations, active operations by our troops will be suspended as from noon, Monday 11 July.

The bi-lateral truce came into being after some three years of relentless guerrilla warfare by the IRA, not just against the British themselves but against all who supported the British presence in Ireland.

The communiqué was the first official intimation of a cease-fire received by many in the IRA who were surprised and discontented by the calling of a truce. One of the active commanders, a young man named Ernie O'Malley, with an excellent record in the war, wrote to a fellow officer on 15 July:

> What do you think of the Peace Move? There seems to be something in it whatever it is. Perhaps Dev [Eamon de Valera] would accept a Republic with the exclusion of Ulster. We are very much worried as we don't know what way the game is going. The number of real Republicans even in the IRA is small — that is of men who will see the Republic through to the bitter end.

The treaty

The negotiations between British and Irish representatives began in London at 10 Downing Street on 11 October 1921. The Irish delegation was led by Arthur Griffith and included Michael Collins who attracted some special but not unpleasant media coverage because he was a former Irish 'terrorist' with a price on his head. Collins commanded an élite IRA hit squad which struck hard at the British military presence generally and at the British intelligence services in particular, throughout the 1919-21 hostilities.

The British invitation for talks did not mention the Dail. Dail Eireann had been proscribed by them as an 'illegal national assembly of the Irish Republic'. No credentials on behalf of an Irish Republic were presented by the five Irish delegates when they came to discuss a settlement. British Prime Minister Lloyd George always talked of negotiating with Sinn Fein just as with any other Irish political party, and never with elected representatives of an existing Irish Republic.

The British conditions from the start were inflexible. Ireland had to remain in the empire and 'Ulster' must not be coerced.

The treaty allowed for a self-governing dominion of 26 counties only, and within the British empire. The new Irish Free State would be permitted its own, but limited army, autonomy in internal affairs and, in theory, control over its own revenues. It would *not* be a republic.

Members of the Free State parliament would have to take oaths to the British monarch. The monarch would appoint a governor-general to reside in Dublin. British forces would keep strategic harbours and no Irish navy would be permitted, for 'security reasons'. And there were other tangible restrictions.

Acceptance of the treaty meant abandonment of the Irish Republic which the Easter Rising had proclaimed and which had been democratically and constitutionally ratified by Dail Eireann in January 1919. Griffith and Collins never seriously pressed the issue of the Republic, and the absent de Valera was ambivalent about it.

Griffith conceded to Lloyd George that six counties in the north could opt out of a united Ireland. Lloyd George promised that there would be a boundary commission which could adjust the border 'in accordance with the wishes of the inhabitants, so far as may be compatible with economic and geographic conditions.' Michael Collins assumed such a commission would give all of Tyrone and Fermanagh, plus parts of Derry, Armagh and Down to Dublin rule. He put his faith in the British government, or perhaps simply in himself.

The treaty was signed in London by the British and Irish delegates on the night of 5-6 December 1921, after two months of talks and under Lloyd George's sudden threat of 'immediate and terrible war' if the treaty was not signed that same night.

Later, in the ensuing Dail debates as to whether to approve the treaty or not, many of the TDs (elected members of the Dail) claimed that it gave the people what they wanted. In reality it meant a glorified form of Home Rule at best. Ireland was left under the British crown, including an oath of allegiance to be taken to King George, his heirs and successors, and to add insult to injury the Irish state was required to vote an annual sum towards the royal revenues. Moreover, the treaty cemented the 1920 Act which had partitioned the country.

The British, however, were jubilant. Lloyd George told his cabinet that 'the terms of the oath to be taken by members of the Parliament of the Irish Free State are remarkable and are better in many respects than the terms of the Oath of Allegiance ordinarily required in Great Britain.' Lord Curzon was gratified that the settlement was 'an astonishing victory for the Empire which would have incalculable effects throughout the whole world and in particular would remove a dark cloud which had hung for years over Great Britain's relations with the United States of America.'

The British had got what they wanted by exploiting already existing divisions. The Dail began a series of bitterly divisive debates.

For treaty and Free State

One most important factor in the signing of the treaty was the presence of Arthur Griffith in the Irish delegation sent to London to negotiate. It was Griffith, the founder of Sinn Fein, who was first to sign his name to Lloyd George's treaty proposals on that crisis night in December 1921. Ironically, others coming into his party from the older republican traditions had made of his Sinn Fein something he had never intended, making it much more radical. Griffith had said openly that he was 'a King, Lords and Commons man'. To him, Irish freedom meant freedom for Irish industrialists to manoeuvre to greater advantage within the imperial system. An independent republic had no place in his mind. His part in the treaty settlement was logical and consistent. He had always supported capitalist interests, even calling in 1911 for British forces to break a workers' strike led by Larkin and Connolly.

The second Irishman to sign the treaty was Michael Collins. A big man, in more than the physical sense, he was probably the dominating personality in the national acceptance of the treaty's articles. He had held high positions in both the IRA and the underground Republican

Members of the Irish delegation in London for the treaty discussions. Seated l. to r. they are: Arthur Griffith, Eamon Duggan, Michael Collins and Robert Barton. Standing is George Gavan Duffy (with beard). They would eventually sign the treaty without reference back to Dublin.

government during the 1919-21 Anglo-Irish war, but during the London talks the British establishment had worked on him as they did not need to work on Griffith, until he too agreed that an independent Irish Republic was no longer a current option. Flattery may have helped: the social whirl, the apparent friendships with such notables as Winston Churchill and Lord Birkenhead.

From 1919-21 Michael Collins had been fully engaged in an inevitably bloody guerrilla war and without a 'democratic mandate', something which was conveniently overlooked when like many another after him he became a 'statesman' in imperialist power games. Ironically, a year earlier the British believed that Eamon de Valera was a moderate who would accept less than an independent republic (and were not so far wrong) but saw Collins as a dangerous extremist.

The personality and influence of Collins helped to coin the phrase 'What's good enough for Mick Collins is good enough for me', and many in the IRA ranks, especially from his own Cork county, believed his word that the treaty was but a stepping stone to the Republic. Unhappily, to have called it a millstone would have been nearer the mark.

A strong supporter of the treaty was Richard Mulcahy, the IRA's Chief of Staff during the war and also an elected Sinn Fein member of Dail Eireann. He was the one to whom many politicals looked for military direction, and to whom some of the army looked for political guidance. Mulcahy announced during the treaty debates that in reality the IRA had suffered a defeat — they had not been able to drive the enemy from anything but a fairly good-sized police barracks, so hence the necessity for truce and treaty. Many in the IRA were angered at this dismissal of their efforts, their achievements which had forced the British empire to swallow its pride and talk terms with 'rebels'. However, very few IRA activists were elected representatives to the Dail with a vote on the matter.

One of the leading pro-treatyites, Kevin O'Higgins, interpreted the treaty with total disregard for either its binding legal implications or for the six separated counties of the north by saying: '*It removes all English control or interference within the shores of Ireland.*'

It was disastrous that the Irish Labour party, its vision drastically lowered from James Connolly's plans for a socialist workers' republic, blundered into support for the treaty and the state that it established. Connolly's successors failed to claim any significant part in the 26 counties at that critical time. There was no revolt in the Labour movement even when de Valera issued his '*Labour must wait*' edict on behalf of Sinn Fein. Labour was told to stand aside in the national interest until independence had been won. Instead, very much because of the non-involvement of organised Labour in that struggle, the government that ruled the Free State from 1922 to 1932 would represent the most pro-imperialist elements in the country.

The treaty supporters outside the Dail were all very much to be expected. There were the southern unionists who made the most of a bad situation and shrewdly understood the advantages of this early exercise in neo-colonialism. Their four elected members went into a 26-county parliament whereas they had previously refused to take part in the Dail.

The landed gentry, as ever, knew where their best interests lay. Despite all, their king was still king of Ireland; their peerages, even more importantly their great estates, remained untouched. The terror of a real Irish revolution was gone as soon as the treaty was signed and confirmed. Then all the vested interests of big business followed them in customary fashion.

The academics were not far behind. Professors had their histories to rewrite, a busy occupation. And the intellectuals of the day soon joined them, playing safe as usual. It was usually the last but one republican uprising that got official recognition.

All these categories went into the newly created Senate, an upper house of favour and privilege which was to consent to all the oppressive legislation of the Free State.

As for the press, their reaction could easily be anticipated. After having utterly condemned the Irish Republican Army during its recent war against the British (employing many of the arguments and abuse that are still in use today), they immediately swung round to support IRA and Sinn Fein members who had apparently abandoned 'terrorism' and were now approved of by Winston Churchill and the British newspapers. For weeks during the truce and treaty debates Irish editorials and articles were pressurising public opinion with headlines as simple as 'Rejection and Chaos', 'Ratification or Ruin'.

And in Catholic Ireland the clergy made the most of the Christmas season and pounded their pulpits to good effect. The Roman Catholic bishops were authoritarian, but the British were mistaken when they suspected that many priests were republican sympathisers.

Further backing for the treaty and its promises came from the middle classes, generally neutral in the recent war and making up a large slice of the electorate.

Then there were the ever-present pro-British elements throughout Irish society, including soldiers from the First World War's disbanded regiments. Many of them transferred their allegiance to the treaty-established state and enlisted to fight against its 'rebels'. (Today the

British army still retains specifically Irish regiments, recruited from south and north, such as the Irish Rangers, who are not required to 'serve' in Northern Ireland, and the Irish Guards, to whom royalty presents shamrock on St Patrick's day.)

Others who had fought and had given, supported or suffered, were naturally war-weary. It had been a brutal struggle. And there were those who were genuinely confused or repulsed by the leadership disputes.

When the Dail vote on whether or not to accept the treaty was eventually taken on 7 January 1922, after long and bitter speeches in debate, it was after the Christmas recess. The interval worked in favour of the pro-treatyites. Delay permitted second thoughts, following on much favourable international opinion of the British 'deal'.

The vote for acceptance was 64 to 57, even though only three of the 64 were positively in favour. The others said they agreed only to avoid the British threats of renewed war. With just a few votes the other way the British bluff would have been called.

The 64 were satisfied, and the other 57 walked out.

Republicans

The first to reject the treaty were the activists of the recent war. Although not all military leaders would remain in the IRA to fight against the Free State, many of the best of them did, such as Tom Barry and Ernie O'Malley who were field commanders. Some of them suspected the motives of certain GHQ staff, believing they used high army rank to further political ambitions in a non-Republican Ireland. Then there were idealists, always a considerable force in the movement, and the separatists, those who believed with Wolfe Tone, a founder of Irish republicanism in the late 18th century, that 'the connection between Ireland and England [is] the curse of the Irish nation and [feel] that while it lasted this country could never be free or happy.'

Certainly there was an economic root to the struggle. Most of the republicans came from the rural and urban poorer class levels, but unfortunately they had not given much previous thought to winning over the vital support from the people of no property, and during the civil war they would have insufficient time or opportunity to do so.

Yet socialist ideals were always acceptable in the IRA, ever since James Connolly's Citizen Army had fused with the Irish Volunteers on Easter Monday 1916 to form the one army of the Irish Republic proclaimed on that day. However, during the war with Britain that followed there were those at General Headquarters who were hostile to such ideology. When Irish workers in the south and south-west were inspired by the Russian revolution and took over businesses and creameries in order to set up their own soviets and co-operatives, or when landless people tried to take over ranches and desmesnes, the Dublin GHQ ordered local IRA units to stop them. But IRA leaders who took the Republican side in the civil war, such as Tom Barry and Peadar O'Donnell, supported land redistribution.

A great Republican support came from women. The 1916 Easter proclamation had been addressed to both sexes. The Cumann na mBan was a woman's army whose members wore uniforms and used guns. Republican women were elected to the Dail, not simply as widows of murdered husbands but in their own right, and all the women TDs strongly opposed the treaty and voted against it. The tradition continued, with women taking part in the military and political wings of the movement.

Also involved were the very young. Those too young to have fought against Britain followed their elders into the Republican ranks. Boys of 15 and 16 were imprisoned by the Free State during the civil war; at least one hut in a major internment camp was reserved for those under eighteen.

An especially potent background to the Republican cause was the fervent support given by relatives of the executed dead of 1916: from Pearse's mother and sister, from Connolly's wife and daughters, from brothers, sisters, children and widows of the rest. This support established a link with the latest of the Irish uprisings.

Liam Mellows and Constance Markievicz were the only participants in the treaty debates to speak for working class interests. However, Mary MacSwiney called Lloyd George 'the most unprincipled scoundrel in history' and begged the Dail not to be fooled by him. She warned that if the Dail accepted the treaty, Ireland would abandon the anti-imperialist struggle, leaving India and Egypt to battle the British empire alone.

Constance Markievicz, born a Gore-Booth, was the daughter of Anglo-Irish aristocrats and the wife of a Polish count. Dressed in her green Cumann na mBan uniform, she told the Dail that she stood for Connolly's Workers' Republic for which she had fought in 1916. An angry TD shouted in abuse: 'Soviet Republic!' She persisted:

> a state run by the Irish people for the people. That means a
> government that looks after the rights of the people before the rights of
> property. ... My idea is the Workers Republic for which Connolly died.
> And I say that this is one of the things that England wishes to prevent.

She pointed out that 'English imperialism' was working 'by a change of names.'

Above: like other released prisoners of the 1916 Easter rising, Constance Markievicz was greeted by huge crowds in Dublin in 1917.

It is the capitalist interests in England and Ireland that are pushing this treaty to block the march of the working people in England and Ireland.

Countess Markievicz was Minister for Labour in the Dail. In 1918 she had been the first woman ever to be elected to the British House of Commons, but in true Sinn Fein fashion had refused to take her seat. She had also been in a British prison at the time. Her constituency was a poor Dublin working class area, which supported her to the end of her life.

In the Dail debates she objected to 'a deliberate attempt to set up a privileged class.' She also agreed with a proposal to give land to IRA men

19

with farming experience and urged 'that some land be given to women, who are just as capable of running farms as men are.'

Liam Mellows, who had also taken part in the Easter Rising, made one of the most valuable contributions to the debates. He explained the British thinking behind the treaty:

> If they [the Irish] divide on this, we can let them fight it out, and we will be able to hold the country; if they accept, our interests are so well safe-guarded that we can still afford to let them have it.

He was also prophetic:

> The government of the Free State will eventually occupy the same relationship towards the people of Ireland as Dublin Castle does today, because it will be the barrier government between the British and the Irish people. And the Irish people before they can struggle on, will have to do something to remove that Free State government...

There was little debate about partition and the Ulster situation, chiefly because de Valera had effectively agreed with Collins's strategy to put reliance on the future Boundary Commission, while continuing to speak out for the nationalists and reinforce the IRA in the north. At private cabinet discussions, even before negotiations began, de Valera had said: 'I want to eliminate the Ulster question out of it.' He would accept terms regarding Northern Ireland for the sake of 'internal peace', saying, 'Let us not start to fight with Ulster.'

He opposed the treaty basically because he considered that a better bargain could have been negotiated. He tried unsuccessfully to propose a compromise solution in the Dail, known as document No.2, which would allow for some ill-defined form of 'external association' with the United Kingdom. Griffith called it a quibble over words and many Republicans agreed with him.

There was one Dail motion proposed by a woman TD who sought to extend the franchise to younger women, but Griffith said that such a decision would 'torpedo the treaty' and it was lost by nine votes.

Two armies

The Irish Republican Army's allegiance was to the Irish Republic as proclaimed at Easter Week 1916, yet it had also acknowledged the authority of Dail Eireann. Two clearly opposing views quickly emerged: one, that a decision made by the elected representatives of the Irish people by however small a majority had to be accepted by the army; the other, that by disestablishing the Republic which the IRA was sworn to defend, the Dail had no longer any right to its allegiance.

The women's branch of the republican army was even more resolute. At a special February conference of Cumann na mBan, Mary MacSwiney proposed a motion reaffirming allegiance to the Republic and denouncing the London agreement. It was passed overwhelmingly.

As early as January 1922 it seemed likely that an independent Republican headquarters staff would be set up, but Liam Lynch of County Cork opposed such a move and as his command was strongest numerically the others would not break away without him. A full army convention was called for in two months' time, an arrangement which suited Defence Minister Richard Mulcahy as it allowed him to consolidate the pro-treaty position. Mulcahy also insisted that the forthcoming March convention should be held only by permission of the cabinet.

A regular army was essential to uphold the prestige and authority of the new government and to prevent 'the mutinous section of the IRA' making too much headway. Mulcahy began to recruit first from the 'old IRA' in dependable areas such as Dublin, Meath, Carlow and Longford.

The first serious military crisis occurred in the key city of Limerick in March 1922. Its strategic position could well divide pro-government western and southern forces. The government's plan was for 'loyal' detachments of the 1st Western Division to move into the city and take over evacuated British barracks because the local IRA brigades had repudiated Dublin's political control.

When the pro-treaty troops made their move into Limerick, the Republicans rushed into the city from many outlying areas and intended confrontation. However, Liam Lynch used his IRB relationship with Dublin GHQ to bring about a compromise, so that government soldiers and those Republicans from outside the area agreed to withdraw, but the local IRA units remained. It suited Mulcahy's purposes to not yet force the issue, although his Department of Defence report on the crisis was one of total condemnation:

> The Limerick episode disclosed the extent to which even as early as the beginning of February, the movement to split the Army had gone and the extent to which those who were driving this split were prepared to go.

The Limerick crisis took place in Ernie O'Malley's area. He was then commanding the 2nd Southern Division. Numbering about 13,000, it was the second largest of the IRA divisions. Mulcahy's February reference in his report explicitly related to the 2nd Southern. In February, O'Malley and his four brigades had made an historic break with the pro-treaty

GHQ and *also* renounced all former allegiance to the democratically elected Dail Eireann because that body had voted for the treaty. Not long afterwards the rest of the Republican Army followed that lead, and the IRA were to reject political control and to continue an independent course of action throughout most of the years that have followed.

Arthur Griffith made the Limerick danger point an excuse to forbid the IRA convention which was due to be held the same month, because he and his government rightly feared the independent spirit of the army. It was announced that any in the IRA who attended the banned convention would be dismissed from the (official) army. Yet the convention was held as planned on 26 March and it was estimated that about 75 per cent of the IRA was represented by the 211 delegates who unanimously approved a resolution that reaffirmed the army's allegiance to the Irish Republic. This defiance hastened the full creation of a government army, and mass recruitment especially amongst the out-of-work population and ex-British soldiers went ahead urgently.

Meanwhile those IRA members who supported the convention set up their own GHQ staff and reorganised ranks by rejecting some former leaders and comrades in order to remain the army of the Republic. Liam Lynch was elected as Chief of Staff. Some of the old GHQ had stayed Republican and they formed part of the new staff; amongst them were Rory O'Connor and Liam Mellows. For a headquarters the new Republican Executive took over the Four Courts in Dublin. The Four Courts was the seat of (British) justice in Ireland; its distinguished Georgian buildings contained the main law courts and occupied a whole block of streets beside the river Liffey. Republican soldiers entered the Courts late one April night and there they remained, since the Dublin government was not yet strong enough to deal with them, much as it wished to do so. And so, despite angry rumblings in British circles and the Irish press, the Republicans maintained their garrison within the justice buildings and became more than a symbolic focus for those Irish men and women who would say with their Chief of Staff Lynch: 'We have declared for an Irish Republic and will not live under any other law.'

The other Irish army, that under the direction of Mulcahy, recruited and trained with the help of British recognition and support. When British troops evacuated military barracks in country areas, the posts were often taken over by Republican units since much depended on local attitudes and most of the divisions and independent brigades were still led by IRA commanders. However, the important Dublin barracks were handed direct to Mulcahy's men, some of whom first called themselves (unofficially) the 'Official IRA', until all realised how inappropriate, how ludicrous indeed, was such a name for the Free

One supposed advantage of the treaty was the evacuation by the British of most of their barracks in the 26 counties. British troops marched out, and pro-Free State troops marched in.

State's army within the British empire. So instead they became known as the 'National Army'. There was increasing friction between the two armies, especially in the country parts where republicanism had flourished and resistance had been strong against Britain.

The ultimate — and ironic — abuse came when the government, its army, the press, the clergy, and consequently most of the general public, no longer recognised the existence of the Irish Republican Army. It was as though the IRA had vanished overnight. The treaty had ignored the claims of the Irish Republic and of course there could be no place for a republican army in the Free State. Yet many from government and from the new army had once been in the IRA, and the IRA was organised on the same lines as before, and with exactly the same antecedents. But instead the thousands of IRA soldiers were labelled by Free State propaganda 'the Irregulars'; the media followed suit, and although they would be called worse names as the civil war progressed, this name was to them the most insulting. As much resented as when freedom fighters are tagged as terrorists.

Overleaf: the establishment press was virtually united in supporting the treaty, so republicans often had to express their opposition through leaflets and posters.

Think, People, Think

Do YOU thoroughly UNDERSTAND the Issue?

Are you, by your Free Vote, going to disestablish the Republic of Ireland for which many brave young men have DIED, and for which Thousands of our Countrymen have risked all, to uphold,

REMEMBER—this will be the Immediate Result

of the Establishment of a Free State Government

The glorious achievements of our "Flying Columns" under most trying circumstances, and against such fearful odds, can find no parallel in the World's history; nor can any future generation of TRUE Irishmen fail to remember or glory in the deeds of such Heroes. Some have nobly perished, but—

What did they FIGHT AND DIE FOR?

Was it that Ireland, by foregoing her claim as a Sovereign State, should accept as a Final Settlement a status less than that of a British Dominion, and thereby strenghten the position of the British Empire to our own detriment?

UNDOUBTEDLY NO! and the person who states that these men laboured for any other purpose but the upholding of the IRISH REPUBLIC, established in 1916, is but trying to belie his own conscience.

Will YOU be a party to lowering the Flag of the

Republic, stained only by the Blood of Irish Martyrs?

By recording your Vote for the Free State, you are, perhaps unconsciously, doing your utmost to tighten the bonds of slavery on our Country, and future generations shall curse those responsible for surrendering our position at a most unique moment. Remember, there will not, and cannot, be peace in Ireland until the might of the British Empire has vanished in every form from our sight.

A COLLECTION will be made throughout the Constituency of South Cork for the purpose of defraying Expenses in connection with the General Election

Rally to the Standard of the Republic!

Long Live the Republic!

Governments and pacts

As civil war drew near, there already was a newly established government in the 26 counties which was backed by British power and influence. This gave the pro-Free State authorities an immediate and immense advantage.

Eamon de Valera had resigned after losing the treaty vote and had been replaced as president by Arthur Griffith. The anti-treaty Sinn Fein members had nowhere to go politically. They had rejected the Free State concept and could only await the intended summer election.

Michael Collins became chairman of the Provisional Government that took over from the British administration and in the following months he used his control of the Irish Republican Brotherhood to win support from substantial sections of the IRA and Sinn Fein. A conspiratorial movement was used to swing over politically inexperienced men and women. Collins, between January and June 1922, acted more as a leader of the IRB than a leading minister of a constitutional government.

He had, however, also to consider the other part of the country. The first Craig-Collins pact was signed in London on 21 January 1922. Collins undertook to lift a damaging boycott of northern goods in return for Craig's pledge 'to facilitate in every possible way' the return of Catholic workers to the Belfast shipyards from which they had been expelled. The boundary question soon predominated, with Craig objecting that Collins had shown him maps which indicated that 'he [Collins] has already promised to bring into the Free State almost half the area of Northern Ireland.'

A more wide-ranging Craig-Collins agreement was signed on 30 March 1922 in London by representatives of the three governments. It was entitled 'An Agreement between the Provisional Government and the Government of Northern Ireland' and so amounted to a formal recognition of the six counties state. It began: *'Peace is today declared.'*

Almost immediately afterwards Craig refused an inquiry into the latest murders of Catholics in Belfast and Collins then broke off any practical co-operation. Large areas of Belfast during the spring and summer of 1922 were virtually at war. Thousands of nationalist refugees streamed across 'the border', having been burned out of their homes and attacked by loyalist mobs, or simply fleeing through a real fear of the outcome. Most of the Northern IRA stayed loyal to the Provisional Government in Dublin. Their defences were so weak that they believed their best hope lay in political and military support from Collins and his cabinet. Meanwhile the Catholic minority in the north abstained from

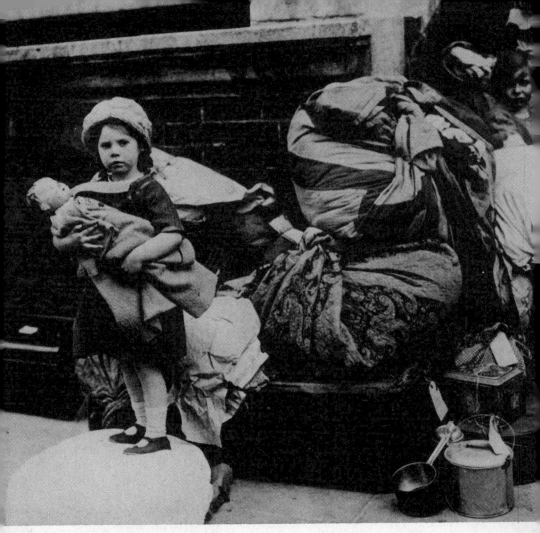

Loyalist pogroms in the north forced thousands of nationalists to flee their homes. Many of the refugees crossed the border.

local and central government activities, and in the 26 counties the 'Belfast boycott' continued, whereby unionist commercial interests were seriously undermined. Winston Churchill — then in Lloyd George's Liberal cabinet — reacted in typical English Tory mood by describing the boycott as 'merely a blind suicidal contribution to the general hate.'

The British continued to evacuate their military garrisons throughout the 26 counties in accordance with the more palatable terms of the treaty and even Dublin Castle, symbolic seat of power, was duly handed over to Collins. Nonetheless, the British presence was maintained, also in accordance with the treaty. Their political agent, Cope, remained in Dublin to send back his reports. Their military commander, General Macready, kept a watchful eye on the situation.

For a time in the late spring of 1922 the British were uneasy. They were none too sure of their as yet unborn Free State and were alarmed whenever some of the opposing groups seemed to be seeking some kind of compromise agreement. Churchill complained to the British cabinet as late as May 1922:

> There is really none too much difference between the Free State and the Republican parties, and there is general reluctance to kill one another.

June 1922 was a crisis month. First came a general election on 16 June that was to confirm the Free State constitution. Collins and de Valera had signed their own pact in May, calling for a panel of candidates. The election was expected to produce a coalition government of pro and anti-treaty Sinn Fein, as well as allowing for an Army Council of eight, four Republican and four Free State, so as to reunite the IRA.

The British-dictated constitution was published in Ireland only on election day itself, even though Collins had pledged it would be known 10 days before. It was too late for the voters to make their own assessments, particularly people outside Dublin who had even less chance of reading the document in advance of casting their vote. Neither was there universal suffrage because only men over 25 and women over 30 had the franchise. It was also said that during the British war years many republicans had prudently avoided putting their names on crown registers.

The results of the election, conducted by proportional representation, were 58 pro-treaty Sinn Fein, 35 anti-treaty Sinn Fein, 4 Unionists, 17 Labour, 7 Farmers and 17 Others.

The pro-treaty victory looks impressive, yet it was very likely boosted when only two days before the election Michael Collins abandoned his pact with de Valera. Collins had been called to London several times during the campaign. When he returned from his last meeting with the British cabinet, he renounced without any prior warning the electoral pact that he had himself arranged. The short-lived pact had been intended to preserve some fiction of unity between the opposing parties. Griffith had always opposed it. Now the British had persuaded Collins that there should be no alliance or agreement whatsoever with the Republican opposition, not even with a self-confessed non-doctrinaire republican like de Valera.

The IRA's June convention

Liam Lynch had been the only member of the IRB Supreme Council to oppose the treaty provisions in a vote taken in December 1921. Despite this vote, and despite the subsequent ratification of the treaty in the Dail, Lynch and other IRB people on the Republican side maintained close contact with IRB men like Collins and Mulcahy on the pro-treaty side. Negotiations to 'restore unity' continued through the spring and even following the outbreak of war. This annoyed not only non-IRB Republicans who saw the futility of such negotiations and the fact that they were quickly losing the military superiority they had once held, but also pro-treaty officers, also non-IRB, who believed that those protracted negotiations and compromises with their 'enemy', thanks to the IRB old boy network, were impeding the development of a strong pro-treaty army.

Two days after the June 1922 general election, the IRA delegates met for their third convention since the truce almost a year before. It took place in a crisis atmosphere, one of disillusion and anger, and the moderates who still hoped for army reunification were unpopular.

Liam Lynch still believed that the government and its own GHQ could be trusted in negotiations, but many of the delegates saw the vital question as being Republican control of the army and opposition to the treaty.

After some debate, Tom Barry proposed that instead of discussing the reunification ideas any further, the convention should instead consider a motion: 'that an ultimatum be given to Great Britain to withdraw all troops from Ireland within 72 hours', which meant war in the north.

The motion was opposed by Lynch and most of his 1st Southern delegates, but supported by other IRA leaders who opposed the ongoing negotiations between senior IRB members on each side to achieve unity based on compromise.

On a show of hands the motion appeared to have been carried, but a poll was demanded, resulting in 103 for the motion and 118 against. The minority then left the convention and returned to the Four Courts, excluding Lynch and those others who supported him.

The IRA executive was split, the anti-treaty section of the Army was split, and the convention broke up in gloom and confusion. The Dublin and London governments received full reports of the discussions.

The shooting of Wilson

On 22 June 1922 Field Marshal Sir Henry Wilson, former Chief of the Imperial General Staff, was shot dead outside his London house by two Irish men. Wilson was a most influential Irish Unionist, with a distinct hatred for all things pertinent to Irish independence. He was considered responsible for the pogroms against the Catholic nationalist minority in Belfast. Before that, in 1920, he had objected to unauthorised reprisals carried out by British troops in the 26 counties only because: 'If these men [IRA and civilians] ought to be murdered, then the government ought to murder them.'

'If we don't reinforce Ireland by every available man, horse, gun, aeroplane, that we have got in the world we would lose Ireland at the end of this summer, and with Ireland the Empire'.
Sir Henry Wilson, May 1921

Field Marshal Sir Henry Wilson was Chief of the Imperial General Staff from 1918-1922. He was then elected Unionist MP for North Down and became security adviser to the Northern Ireland government. He was considered responsible for the pogroms against Catholics.

It has been generally accepted that the killing of Wilson was carried out by order of Michael Collins. The two Irish who were captured on the spot (and hanged a few weeks later) were Collins's own men. Collins's own motives still remain obscure. He might have wanted to placate his followers in the six Ulster counties whom the treaty he signed had abandoned, or he might have been trying to beat the British at their own game of duplicity.

The consequence was that the British immediately chose to blame the IRA, in particular the garrison holding the Four Courts buildings in Dublin.

General reaction to the shooting of Wilson was extreme horror and outrage on both sides of the Irish Sea. Shock and condemnation were stressed as vigorously as only newspapers know how for public consumption. Arthur Griffith, who never dreamed that his partner Collins was deeply implicated, was appalled and sent telegrams of sympathy to King George and to Wilson's family.

But Britain was demanding more than sympathy. Its government wanted the defeat of those who were opposing their plans for Ireland and that meant the destruction of the Republican headquarters in Dublin's Four Courts. The pro-treaty government had long shared the same wish. Thus the result of the Wilson assassination was to turn the full force of British and Irish governments against the IRA, even though the IRA strongly denied having anything to do with his death, and their publicity department issued the following statement:

> The shooting of Sir Henry Wilson was not done at the insistence of the IRA. If it were, the IRA would acknowledge the fact. The death of Sir Henry Wilson is to be deplored not because it occurred apparently at the hands of Irishmen, but because he is the victim of the imperial policy pursued by the British Government in Ireland... It would be hypocritical to condemn such actions as the shooting of Wilson while the causes that provoke such deeds remain.

Decision to attack

Lloyd George stated in the House of Commons that he did not want to use 'the language of menace' but that it was essential that the 'sham Government and organised force' in the Four Courts should be brought to an end, 'and speedily'. Churchill added his own threat that if the 'band of men' were not removed, 'then it is my duty, on behalf of His Majesty's Government, to say that the Treaty has been formally violated.'

For a few days the British were seriously prepared to take the Four Courts with the use of their own troops, in what would have been a total disregard of the treaty. Then they realised how very much better it would be if the pro-treaty government in Dublin were to do the work for them. The British preference was always to use the 'economy' of Irish lives to preserve their own influence. Accordingly pressure was renewed on Dublin and, once they had received British promises of heavy gun artillery and military advice, Dublin was ready to use its newly-formed army against those former companions in arms who had rejected the Free State and continued to stand for a fully independent Ireland.

Arthur Griffith's cabinet needed little coercion to move against their Republican opponents. One witness remembered seeing Griffith hitting the table with his fist and shouting, '*Now* we must act against them!'

A final excuse was needed for the British demand to be met and this was soon forthcoming. On 26 June, four days after Wilson was shot, Leo Henderson was arrested in Dublin by government troops while he was commandeering cars to be used in raids on the north. He was the Republican GHQ's director of the Belfast boycott and by arresting him the Dublin government broke faith over similar such actions they had previously ignored in the name of support for northern nationalists. Henderson was hauled off to jail as a common criminal.

In response, and it was his own idea, Ernie O'Malley went out from the Four Courts and arrested the government's Assistant Chief of Staff, J.J. O'Connell, who was then held as hostage for the release of Henderson. One Irish Free State minister later called this incident the 'mini-Sarajevo' of the civil war. Government propaganda claimed they reacted only to this 'kidnapping' of their general and not because of British demands for action, but the decision to attack the Courts had already been made.

Apart from British pressure, the timing of the attack was influenced by the recent IRA convention split. But Griffiths and Collins did not know that Lynch had just mended the rift by agreeing to resume as Chief of Staff. Even so, Lynch and other Cork commanders did not remain in the Courts but left for the south, without hindrance from government forces.

The Four Courts

At about 4 a.m. on 28 June 1922 the bombardment of the Four Courts announced to the city the beginning of civil war. In Republican history the Four Courts in June 1922 stands out as a symbol as significant as the General Post Office at Easter 1916. Both buildings were military headquarters for the men and women fighting to establish or to defend the Irish Republic, and when both were destroyed by superior enemy power the struggle only intensified. But in 1922 it was Irish people, including former comrades, who attacked other Irish people and they were using borrowed English guns to do it. The British commander-in-chief, General Macready, had supplied the artillery and British officers were available to instruct but otherwise stayed discreetly in the background.

For two days the Courts was shelled by heavy 18-pounders and its garrison of about 150 were surrounded by troops of the 'national' army, whose new green uniforms were modelled on the British style.

The Republican headquarters at the Four Courts was shelled to destruction by a new Irish army using borrowed British guns.

Republicans already called these pro-treaty troops by the contemptuous term of 'Staters'.

The newly elected Dail was due to assemble on 30 June, but the Dublin government postponed it indefinitely because of the war situation. Its usefulness to them would come later.

About 11.30 a.m. on the day that the Dail was due to reassemble, there occurred one of the great explosions that go down in history. The IRA garrison had stored mines, explosives and quantities of TNT inside the Courts so that when the shelling started a fierce fire, the end result was predictable. Most of one main building and part of another went up in flames and smoke, with a great pall of darkened air hanging over the city. The Four Courts was not only the centre of Anglo-Irish 'justice' in Ireland but housed the legal and national archives. Hundreds of books and records went hurtling across the sky. Some papers landed miles away. Ernie O'Malley had been standing by an outer gate at the moment of explosion and he later recalled how everything shook around him in a blast of hot air and a book fell at his feet. It was an account of the secret service money paid to informers after the 1798 rebellion, and he wondered whether in another hundred years there would be any records available of similar secret money paid out in 1922.

Surprisingly no one was badly hurt but undoubtedly the garrison's morale was affected. They were also running very short of ammunition and food. The Dublin government demanded and received the same kind of surrender as the British government had obtained in 1916 – total and unconditional. Afterwards the Republicans were marched away to the old British prison of Mountjoy but a few of them escaped on the way, one of them being O'Malley.

A major weakness in the Republicans' defence of the Courts had been the presence there of most of the GHQ staff, so that offensive measures planned by the garrison commander, and then his intention to evacuate, were over-ruled in favour of a symbolic gesture of resistance. Another major factor in defeat was the military tactics of the IRA Dublin brigade who took up positions on the wrong side of O'Connell Street so that they could not break through to the Courts and became isolated themselves.

A week of intense fighting took place in Dublin, mostly around O'Connell Street, and for the second time in a few years much of the city centre was devastated. The Staters sprayed buildings with petrol and set them alight. When it was over, many of the Republicans had escaped out of the capital but one of their best-known leaders, Cathal Brugha, had been killed after refusing to surrender.

The Republicans kept a semi-underground political party, the anti-treaty Sinn Fein TDs, but were deprived of any official recognition. Some TDs were either in prison, in the IRA, or in exile. Eamon de Valera, the party's president and a bourgeois politician by instinct and practice, was in hiding and apart from the military contest of which he hardly approved.

The British and the north

The British, of course, remained in that part of Ulster to be ruled by the new Stormont (six county) parliament and active assistance was given to the Free Staters in adjoining areas.

The old, all-Ireland police force, hitherto called the Royal Irish Constabulary, had been split by the act of partition into the Garda Siochana for the 26 counties and the (slightly renamed) Royal Ulster Constabulary for the other six. There was a mutual exchange of prisoners along the new border and in Britain many suspected Republican sympathisers, Irish men and women, were rounded up and deported to Dublin where they were promptly interned without trial.

The outbreak of civil war relieved the Northern Ireland government of critical pressure and allowed them to take extremely repressive measures against the nationalist population. The result in the north was a comparative but not a permanent peace. From Belfast, Joe Devlin's nationalist constitutionalist party was backed by the conservative Catholic Church. On 4 July 1922 the Belfast-based Catholic Protection Committee congratulated the Dublin government for its attack on the Four Courts and wished it 'God speed' in its efforts.

Press control

The main Republican paper was *An Phoblacht* (*The Republic*). It began in January 1922 and continued sporadically over the years despite many attempts to suppress it. From the start it was constantly raided, its presses destroyed and the staff arrested, just as in earlier times the British had hunted for rebellious publications. Because of the rigid censorship, slogans were painted around Dublin: 'CALL OFF THE MURDER GANG', 'YOU HAVE MURDERED PRISONERS', 'UP THE REPUBLIC'.

The Free Staters by contrast enjoyed all the advantages of an official government supported by Britain and the pro-British allies within Ireland, together with general international acceptance. They soon possessed a regular and ever more effective army and a confidence that swelled in proportion to their rapidly mounting hatred for their enemies: a hatred fanned by the rabid anti-republicanism of press and pulpit. And, tragically, because it was a civil war, not just former friends but families were bitterly divided. It was not infrequent for fathers and sons, brothers and sisters, husbands and wives to be active opponents of each other, even those from families who had all been republicans up to 1922. That enmity lasted sometimes just as long amongst individuals as in national politics.

The government had powers to control the press through direct censorship but that course was not usually needed since the newspapers, particularly in Dublin, were quite willing to follow the official line. Some provincial papers did leave blank spaces to show their objections to censorship even at time of war.

Two of the Dublin papers, the *Irish Times* and *Freeman's Journal*, had reluctantly acknowledged an Irish Free State but definitely approved of the tough stand against 'violence' and 'lawlessness'. The conservative 'native' paper, the *Irish Independent*, had been fiercely opposed to the Easter Rising in 1916 and was true to form in 1922. It had welcomed the treaty wholeheartedly and so its campaign was savage against the 'murderers', 'looters', 'bank-robbers', 'criminals', etc., who were endangering the life of the new state by waging armed revolt.

Typical examples of editorial thinking of the time can be found in the *Free State Journal*, a weekly publication that reflected government opinion and often had cabinet ministers writing for it. The *Journal* said on 8 July 1922 just after the fall of the Four Courts:

> To save a Republic that never existed in fact, a number of young men, partly blustering bullies, partly fanatics honest with the terrible honesty of a monomania, partly boys with no mind but for an escapade, broke away from the army of the nation, set themselves up as the directing force of the country, plunder and destroy, threaten and lie, uniting all their diverse qualities of bravado, unreason and irresponsibility to render any government impossible but theirs.

It should be remembered that this was written by, and partly written for, the very people who only six months earlier had professed to believe in the 1916 Republic just as firmly as the persons here condemned. But obviously six months of power had made all the difference.

Later in the year the much more blatant form of military censorship was seen in special instructions sent out to editors and others by the Free State army's publicity department:

1. The Army must always be referred to as the 'Irish Army', the 'National Army', 'National Troops', or simply 'troops'.
2. The Irregulars must not be referred to as the 'Executive Forces', nor described as 'forces' or 'troops'. They are to be called 'bands' or 'bodies' of men.
3. Irregular leaders are not to be referred to as of any rank, such as 'Commandant', etc. or are not to be called officers.
4. Articles or letters as to treatment of the irregular prisoners may not be published.

5. The Censors are not to insert words of their own in any article submitted to them. Their business is to cancel what is objected to. They may, however, propose to substitute words or phrases, such as 'Irregulars' for 'Republicans', 'fired at' for 'attacked', 'seized' for 'commandeered', 'kidnapped' for 'arrested'.

Civil warfare

The Republican forces made the fatal mistake of retreating from Dublin and leaving the capital in the hands of their enemies, thereby allowing the Staters to present themselves to the outside world as the lawful government in general control of the situation.

Throughout July the IRA was consolidating its positions in the country, mostly in the south, with their GHQ in Cork city. Ernie O'Malley remained 'on the run' in Dublin and attempted to build up his Leinster and Ulster commands from there. The Belfast IRA's main activities related to economic warfare, such as the burning and destruction of buildings. They were crushed between British, Unionists and Free Staters, able to make only token resistance and were often so helpless and disorganised that the Belfast OC had to ask Dublin for another map of his city because they had lost the only one they had.

From Mountjoy prison, Liam Mellows, one of the best-known Republican socialists, sent out a smuggled letter to his friend O'Malley, in which he warned:

> No doubt the British will continue to make use of Irishmen if the latter can be duped or dazzled by the Free State idea... For the British to slander Republicans and belittle their cause by besmirching them is one thing. But for Free Staters (and potential Republicans) to do it is another – and different, and worse thing. Because the British will not use British arguments to cloak their actions but Irish ones. 'Out of your own mouths', etc.

In that 1922 summer one leading Republican, Harry Boland, a great friend of Michael Collins, was mortally shot while 'resisting arrest' and other IRA prisoners were murdered in military barracks or gunned down by the roadside. Dublin in 1922 was a city of lorries of troops on the streets, sudden arrests and checkpoints, police raids and brutality. Then the prisons and the camps began to fill. There was a new force, the Criminal Investigation Department; they were armed and carried out raids and interrogations. Soon their headquarters in Dublin, Oriel House, had gained an unsavoury reputation through the work of their heavy gangs. In Dublin there were touts and informers everywhere; the plan was to have two government spies on every street. And so the familiar pattern of repression and violence, and counter-violence and resistance, went on just as if the British were still there. The IRA replied with street ambushes on troops and police, by burning down buildings and seizing mail and money, by local gun battles, the use of mines and bombs, and by ordering that those responsible for the murder and ill-treatment of their soldiers be shot on sight.

Meanwhile the bulk of the Irish Republican Army was holding a southern line from below Limerick across to Cork on the south coast.

Free State troops in action on the streets. Next to them is a republican poster.

There were strong pockets of resistance in the far west, a weaker resistance left in Donegal in north-west Ulster and determined military activity in County Louth along the border, but already after only one month of war the Staters were effectively in control.

Early in August, using a classic strategem, the Free State army attacked by sea, taking the IRA completely by surprise. Free State boats landed troops in Cork harbour and along the Kerry coast and the Republicans fled into the mountains and abandoned their Cork base and gradually what other towns they held. By retreating they seemed to believe that they could fight another successful guerrilla war, but this time the population was war-weary, and they were opposed by an Irish government which had a stronger claim to the allegiance of Irish people than the former British administration. Some kind of semi-open fighting should have been attempted while the IRA was still strong and still sufficiently supported, for eventually it would prove hopeless to wage piecemeal guerrilla warfare against those who had once taken part in such a campaign themselves. However for a while the Cork and Kerry IRA, led by Liam Lynch, were happy to hold the rough country and the wild mountains where they felt at home, while their essential backing from the local population was slowly being eroded.

Deaths of Griffith and Collins

These southern victories helped the Free State to weather the two disasters that suddenly befell it. On 12 August Arthur Griffith died instantly of a brain haemorrhage. Republicans claimed his death was due to shock when he discovered that Collins had been responsible for Henry Wilson's death. The government claimed it was through overwork and years of devoted duty to the nation. Griffith was given a state funeral that eulogized him as a supreme statesman and patriot. The British sent condolences and representatives as marks of respect; the crowds were immense, and according to press reports the whole country was deep in mourning.

Michael Collins was present at the funeral in his brand-new uniform as Commander-in-Chief of the National Army, and contemporary photographs show him as an imposing and dominant figure on the scene. He was also now undisputed head of government in Griffith's place, politically and militarily in control, which hardly pleased all of his colleagues. A few days later he left for a tour of inspection in his native Cork county, and soon after he was dead. He was killed in the course of an ambush on a lonely Cork road when a few IRA men fired on his

Michael Collins and Richard Mulcahy in the military procession at Arthur Griffith's funeral. Ten days after Griffith died, Collins was killed in ambush and Mulcahy became commander-in-chief.

armoured convoy, and his body was brought back to Dublin for a hero's burial. The Free Staters made the most of the widespread grief and shock and the funeral celebrations were splendid and impressive for the one who was now its dead champion, whose name would usefully prop up their role for the future.

But there would always be those who felt that Collins's premature death had prevented any quick or reasonable settlement of the civil war. If he had lived, then possibly the Irish nationalist position would have remained united enough to withstand British pressures, especially with regard to the six northern counties. Others besides the IRA had motives to kill him.

Mulcahy and Cosgrave take over

Griffith and Collins were succeeded by two very different men and from that date there would be no talk of compromise, no thought of going back. William Cosgrave who now became head of government had no great reputation. In a letter from Mountjoy prison, Rory O'Connor, captured after the surrender of the Four Courts, gave this advice:

Cosgrave can be easily scared to clear out. He ran away to Manchester to a priest for seven weeks during the terror [1919-21 war against Britain] and ordered his assistant to close down the Local Government department.

Cosgrave had advanced so far in the political hierarchy because he had been 'out' at Easter 1916, but an eye-witness who noted him in one of the outposts during the Rising recalled:

From what I saw of Cosgrave in the South Dublin Union, saying his Rosary, I'd say he was there by mistake.

The other man who now assumed the real power was of quite different calibre, well suited for his role as what was in practical terms a military dictator (as Collins might have become). Richard Mulcahy was considered by his opponents as cold, humourless and ruthless, and he willingly took on the supreme role. He stepped into Collins's boots and immediately became Commander-in-Chief. He also maintained a political grip by continuing as Minister for Defence in the still unsummoned parliament.

But for a while the Republicans were greatly encouraged by such events. Mick Collins was dead. Dick Mulcahy and Willie Cosgrave were trying to fill his place. Soon fresh slogans began to appear on the walls and pavements of Dublin.

Move over, Mick, make room for Dick,
And Willie follows after.

Republican social policies

In the middle of war some of the military were anxious to think through a socialist programme. Chief of Staff Lynch was not particularly interested in radical politics, but his Assistant Chief of Staff was. One of O'Malley's (unheeded) despatches to Lynch urged:

The need for a Democratic Republican Constitution is felt and I believe it would get the workers. I had a note from the QMG [Patrick

Ruttledge] in which he states that the programme of democratic control adopted by the [First] Dail should be translated into something definite. It would not require change of outlook on the part of Republicans and he suggests that it should be interpreted something on the lines of what appeared in the 'Workers Republic' of July 22, 1922. Under the Republic all industry will be controlled by the State for the workers and farmers benefit; all transport, railways, Canals etc. will be operated by the State – the Republican State – for the benefit of workers and farmers; all banks will be operated by the State for the benefit of industry and agriculture; all loans, mortgages, etc. with the lands of the aristocracy will be seized and divided amongst those who can and will operate it for the owners' benefit.

O'Malley based the despatch on his friend Liam Mellows's notes from Mountjoy jail. Mellows's correspondence was captured in a raid and released to the newspapers by the government under Communist scare headlines. In fact Mellows's intent had been to rally the working class behind the Republic. He had written:

In view of the unprincipled attitude of the Labour Party, and because of the landless and homeless Irish Republican soldiers who fought against Britain, it might be well to publish this scheme in whole or in part. We should certainly keep Irish labour for the Republic; it will be possibly the biggest factor on our side... The 'stake in the country' people were

An IRA patrol on the Donegal-Tyrone border, May 1922.

never with the Republic. They are not with it now – and they will always be against it – until it wins!... The position must be defined. FREE STATE = Capitalism and Industrialism – Empire. REPUBLIC = Workers – Labour.

A priest's recommendations

Father Dominic, one of the few priests who had been imprisoned by the British, wrote to O'Malley in September 1922 about poverty, enemy recruitment, the question of legal authority, and finally but not least the matter of reprisals:

> The destitution amongst our own people is very great, and some funds should be obtained in some way to aid the dependents. Four Courts men are joining the Free State Army because they can get no work and their families are starving. The conditions to which some are reduced is appalling, and yet some of them out of the 5/- per week or 2/6 per week that they get from the Dependents Fund are giving a meal or two to men on the run.
>
> On the few occasions when I had to pass through Brunswick Street I saw a large number of men waiting to join the Free State Army. On inquiring from some of them I discovered that they believed there was very little danger to life or limb and they had a good chance of seeing Ireland and would get good pay. The war, they said, was all over! Might not a few shots be fired over their heads to disperse them and let them see that it is not quite over, and some posters or painted warnings be put up nearby saying all recruits for Free State Army would be treated as enemies attacking the Republic and would be fired on. If they persist, then why not fire, if we are in earnest?
>
> I think it high time to proclaim a Provisional Government of the Republic. It should have been done in January, it was imperative in July and is of the utmost urgency now. We are without a government and are really nothing more in the eyes of the world than "murderers and looters".
>
> And if necessary the Cabinet and its abettors should be wiped out. It is ridiculous to be killing, wounding and maiming private soldiers and under-officers throughout the country and leaving the Cabinet and superior officers severely alone.

'Criminalisation'

Soon there were thousands of prisoners in Free State jails, barracks and internment camps across the country. The Staters had branded the IRA as disorganised bands of criminals without a policy, seeking destruction for destruction's sake and the real enemies of the people of Ireland. Only nine months previously the Free State's leaders had also called themselves Republican, but now they were part of the neo-colonial project in Ireland that the treaty was designed to bring about.

Mass arrests, together with brutality and censorship, made it easier for the government to distort what the prisoners represented. Even daring prison escapes had little impact on the public imagination because they were insufficiently publicised.

The *Free State Journal* of September 1922 carried familiar charges of gangsterism and profiteering, like the 'mafia godfathers' image that the Northern Ireland Office and certain British reporters regularly conjure up today:

Republic or Juggernaut
The Price of Fanaticism

This orgy of death and destruction is perfectly plain to everybody but the mutineers themselves... we turn to examine the psychology that underlies them. And here it will not be amiss to sound a warning for slipshod thinkers who would dispose of the opposition as a band of looters and disappointed men. Undoubtedly every known abuse is sheltering behind their catchcries. Men posing as Republicans are stealing sheep and cattle and living in idleness on the proceeds. Some of the Republican warriors are even starting in business on capital acquired from nowhere within the last few weeks... This is not a war for the Republic; it is a rebellion against the Treaty. It is not holy; it is criminal. It is not just; it is unjustifiable. There is no Republic to be defended, and the oath of allegiance sworn to it by a fraction of the Irish people has no longer any binding force over a single soul.

As Connie Neenan, a Cork IRA veteran, was to say much later about those times:

In the days before December [1921] we were saints and heroes, now we were burglars and bank robbers. We could see it was incomplete and that it would cause endless trouble for generations afterwards – and the North today is proof of that, but the job was to convince people.

The bishops intervene

On 26 April 1922 the Catholic Church hierarchy had again made clear its official position, which was: 'The best and wisest course for Ireland is to accept the treaty and make the most of the freedom it undoubtedly gives us.'

As the Church was backing the new state (just as before it had

It was as if the British had never left. Free State security forces had learnt the lessons well. Above: a taxi is held up at a checkpoint.

accepted integration), it was now judged appropriate for the bishops to pronounce on the moral issues of the war and to bring all their considerable spiritual authority against the 'Irregulars'. A Vatican diplomat returning to Rome after a peace-seeking visit to Ireland was asked if he had met with the Irish bishops. 'I don't know about that,' he replied, 'but I saw seventeen Irish popes.'

Church and state again combined together and in October a solemn pastoral was issued from Maynooth College where the bishops had assembled. Their message was read throughout the nation's churches and was just as well publicised by the state. Part of the pastoral said:

A section of the community, refusing to acknowledge the Government set up by the Nation, have chosen to attack their own country as if she were a foreign power. They have forgotten that a dead nation cannot be free, and have wrecked Ireland from end to end... The guerrilla warfare now being carried on by the irregulars is without moral sanction, and therefore the killing of National soldiers in the course of it is murder before God; the seizing of public and private property is robbery; the breaking of roads, bridges and railways is a criminal destruction; the invasion of homes and the molestation of civilians a grievous crime.

The Republicans were put under General Excommunication and forbidden the use of the Sacraments, so long as they continued to wage war. The bishops had spoken and must have put pressure on waverers, but the majority of the Republican forces had their minds made up and they resented the use of religion for political purposes. If they must die excommunicate, they were ready to die without a bishop's blessing. 'You may or you may nooth' was a joke amongst them and Republican women insulted each other with the cry 'May your son be a bishop!' Whenever British politicians want the Catholic Church to excommunicate the IRA they show their usual ignorance of the Irish past. The Church in Ireland is wiser. When it actually did so excommunicate in the civil war, it had no effect on those who were most involved and only did harm to its own authority and image.

Special emergency powers

When Mulcahy summoned the new parliament to meet for the first time since the summer election, its main business was to confer special powers on his army and to consent to secret military courts that could pass the death sentence on captured Republicans.

No anti-treaty Sinn Fein attended. Token opposition to the Cosgrave party was supplied by the generally compliant Labour party with its 17 TDs. However, when he realised the sweeping emergency powers that Mulcahy was demanding, Labour's leader, Thomas Johnson, was moved to protest that they were being told to agree to a military dictatorship that would have powers of life and death over every civilian in the country.

Mulcahy retorted that only the sniper and the man who went out with a bomb would have reason to fear. When Johnson asked if IRA prisoners would be treated as prisoners of war, Cosgrave said: 'No, certainly not.'

The special act was duly passed with a large majority and came into effect on 15 October 1922. Republicans called it the 'Murder Bill' and threatened all those who voted for it.

Secret military courts would in future deal with those charged with the following offences:

1. Taking part in, or aiding, or abetting any attack upon or using force against the National Forces.
2. Looting, arson, destruction, seizure, unlawful possession, or removal of, or damage to, any public or private property.
3. Having possession without proper authority of any bomb, or article in the nature of a bomb, or any dynamite, or gelignite, or other explosive substance, or any revolver, rifle, gun or other firearm or lethal weapon, or any ammunition for such firearms.

They could impose the following range of penalties:

Death
Penal Servitude
Imprisonment
Deportation
Internment
Fine

Republican government re-formed

Also in October, 11 members of the IRA Executive met secretly in a small village, including Liam Lynch and Ernie O'Malley. Afterwards they issued a proclamation 'in the name of the Army of the Republic':

Last December certain representatives of the nation yielded to English threats of war, violated their pledge and their oaths and entered into an agreement subversive of the independence of the nation and destructive of its territorial integrity. Since that time these representatives and their adherents... have suppressed the legitimate Parliament and judiciary, usurped the Government of the State, and now, by the instigation of the English and with English aid, are endeavouring traitorously to destroy the Republic by force of arms, waging illegal war upon it, and proclaiming death, exile or imprisonment to all its faithful citizens... In these circumstances, in order to preserve the continuity of the independent Irish Government and the better to organise the forces of the Republic in its defence, we, on behalf of the soldiers of the Republic, acting in the spirit of our oath as the final custodians of the Republic... have called upon the former President Eamon de Valera and the faithful members of Dail Eireann, to form a Government, which they have done...

On behalf of the Army, we hereby pledge to that executive our allegiance and our support in all its legitimate efforts to maintain and defend the Republic, and we call upon all our comrades and loyal fellow-citizens and upon our kin throughout the world, to join with us in reasserting our ancient right to be a free people and a free nation, owing allegiance to no foreign authority whatever.

The re-formed government was a government-in-exile in its own country. Forced underground as in the British war, its 12-member Council of State could do little but issue policy documents on an anti-treaty basis. But at least Republicans could claim to have a government once more, and one that derived its authority from the Dail Eireann of the Irish people before the treaty vote was taken.

But this had come too late. Increasingly for the Irish public, the parliament at work in Leinster House, that body set up by Griffith and the British treaty, would appear to be their only logical and therefore legitimate assembly. Over the years its dubious beginnings would be first ignored and then conveniently forgotten.

Eventually the IRA would withdraw its support for de Valera's government because de Valera withdrew from the Republican position. The key phrase in the IRA's 1922 proclamation is *the final custodians of the Republic'*.

The first executions

November 1922 was a bad month for Republicans. Ernie O'Malley, their Assistant Chief of Staff, was captured after a gun battle when troops surrounded a house in the exclusive Dublin suburb which he used as headquarters. He was riddled with bullets and only his severe wounds saved him from sentence of death. He spent more than a year confined to a prison bed and was the last of the IRA commanders to be released when the war was finally over.

Soon after, on 17 November, the Minister for Home Affairs (and Justice) informed the Leinster House assembly that four men had been shot that morning, following a secret court-martial. The first news that the men's relatives received was an official form with the wording 'Remains of ... coffined and buried' and a blank for the name to be inserted. The four were all young IRA volunteers, one of them aged eighteen. It was said that they had been carrying weapons and were planning a street ambush. It was also said that Commander-in-Chief Mulcahy had a special loathing of such methods – a rather strange distaste considering that when he was the IRA Chief of Staff in the British war, his men had made Dublin so dangerous for crown soldiers that the narrow Wexford Street was known as 'the Dardanelles' because of the ambushes that took place there.

These 17 November executions have been called the *hors d'oeuvres* because the man whom the Staters really wanted to kill was standing trial for his life on that same day. So four unknown young men had been shot to prepare the way and condition the public.

The man whom the Staters hated so deeply was the Anglo-Irish Erskine Childers who during the treaty debates had spoken out clearly for the Republic, saying: 'The question is whether Dail Eireann, the national assembly of the people of Ireland, having declared its independence, shall approve of and ratify a treaty relinquishing deliberately and abandoning that independence.' Arthur Griffith in a fury called Childers 'a damned Englishman' although, with one Irish parent, Childers was no less Irish than Pearse, Brugha or de Valera. He

SPECIMEN COPY OF LETTER TO BE SENT TO THE
NEXT-of-KIN OF EACH EXECUTED PRISONER.

I am to inform you that (Name)_____
was tried by_____
that he was found guilty of(Charge)_____
and was sentenced to death.   This sentence was
executed on the morning of_____

                    Respectfully yours,

                    (SIGNATURE)_____

A standard letter intended to be sent to relatives of those prisoners executed by the state during the civil war.

had served well in the British army and navy and in the House of Commons until he accepted that the only way forward for Ireland was through militant republicanism. In 1914 he had brought in guns to help arm the Irish Volunteers, forerunners of the IRA. His belief in the Republic, his intellectual arguments and his committed work in its defence had shamed the Free State establishment.

Because Childers had used his inside knowledge of the British ruling class to warn and advise against them, Britain's propaganda portrayed him as a sinister figure, as a spy, a double-agent, a drug addict, a man who was using Ireland as a catspaw for his own irrational anti-English hatreds. Winston Churchill at once declared that he had:

> seen with satisfaction that the mischief-making murderous renegade, Erskine Childers, has been captured. No man has endeavoured to bring a greater curse upon the common people of Ireland than this strange being. Such as he is may all who hate us be.

It was said that Churchill could have gone closer to home if he were really looking for a rogues' gallery of those who were a curse to what was suddenly his benevolent concern, 'the common people of Ireland.' It was Churchill's own father, Lord Randolph Churchill, who had played the 'Orange card' for his own ends, threatening that 'Ulster will fight and Ulster will be right', and whose selfish political investment haunts both Ireland and Britain today.

A week after his court-martial on charges of possessing a toy-like pistol given to him by Michael Collins in days when they opposed British imperialism together, Erskine Childers was executed by an Irish army squad in a Dublin barracks, even as his appeal was pending. He met death bravely and without bitterness. 'It is 6 a.m. – it all seems perfectly simple and inevitable,' he wrote, 'like lying down after a long day's work.'

'14 Orders of Frightfulness'

The November executions opened a new season of conflict and from then on no captured Republican soldier could be safe from the possibility of the death penalty. When some of the Labour party and some of those labelled as humanitarians again protested at the sentences, especially at the secrecy involved, Mulcahy replied:

> Persons who carry on such work [destroying railways, blocking roads, burning property, etc.] had better settle their private business beforehand. Under present circumstances we do not propose to endeavour to find out who they are or who their people are before we deal with them.

Liam Lynch was shocked by the executions. He had never believed the Free State would actually implement the special powers and he answered Mulcahy with an open communiqué:

> The illegal body over which you preside has declared war on the soldiers of the Republic and suppressed the legitimate parliament of the Irish Nation... We on our side have at all times adhered to the recognised rules of warfare... the prisoners you have taken you have treated barbarously and, when helpless, tortured and murdered them... You now presume to murder the soldiers who had brought Ireland victory when you, traitors, surrendered the Republic twelve months ago. We therefore give you notice that unless your army recognises the rules of warfare in the future, we shall adopt very drastic measures to protect our forces.

When this had no effect whatever, Lynch sent out a special order to his IRA commands in which he listed 14 categories of enemies who were to be dealt with forthwith.

In view of the mass outrage when judges, magistrates, contractors and politicians have been killed in Ireland during the current warfare, and assertions in newspaper editorials that the earlier IRA would never have behaved so murderously, it is interesting to see who Lynch and his officers considered to be legitimate targets in 1922. Then, those to be shot on sight, plus the destruction of their homes or offices, included all members of the Leinster House parliament who had voted for the special emergency powers, hostile newspaper men, editors, High Court judges, senators, and even Unionist representatives and 'aggressive Free State supporters', a term that might encompass anyone. One IRA leader wanted to add on a few bishops as well: Ernie O'Malley considered that they were just as responsible as the cabinet for the savage treatment of prisoners.

The Dublin government denounced the Lynch list as '14 Orders of Frightfulness' but fortunately for them the IRA was already too much on the defensive to be able to carry out most of their Chief of Staff's directives. Few on the list even suffered the loss of homes or property. The campaign of arson was much more widespread than that of attempted assassinations.

The Dublin IRA brigade did make one determined attempt on two Leinster House deputies, killing one of them and seriously wounding the other as they were walking in the street. This happened on 7 December 1922 and resulted in a swift government reprisal that shocked liberal opinion on both sides of the Atlantic.

State terrorism

Once their own lives were plainly in danger, the ordinary Leinster House deputies' support for the government's hardline measures began to waver. Mulcahy and Cosgrave had to move quickly to bring the dangerous new situation under control. One deputy who tried to resign was forced back by threats of treason charges. The government proved itself ruthless in ensuring its own survival.

Mulcahy went to Cosgrave's cabinet and required individual consent to an official reprisal by which four leading Republican prisoners would be summarily executed without formality of trial, although held in prison since the surrender of the Four Courts, months before the special powers had been passed. There was no argument. The cabinet all gave their consent in turn. Eight men around the table consented that the four should die to help guarantee their safety and the safety of their Free State.

And so early in Mountjoy jail next morning, on Sunday 8 December 1922, four men whose names live in Republican memory – Rory O'Connor, Liam Mellows, Joe McKelvey and Dick Barrett – were woken

Liam Mellows.

Rory O'Connor.

Richard Barrett.

Joe McKelvey.

and told that they were to be shot. The 8 December was not just a Sunday, it was the feast of the Immaculate Conception, an important day in the Catholic calendar, but the Cosgrave government did not choose to postpone an action that was meant to shock and to intimidate.

In the dark cold hours the prison chaplain vainly argued with Mellows, trying to force him to accept the bishops' pastoral and confess to the sin of fighting against the Free State, and Mellows refused. 'I believe with the old Gaels, who dies for Ireland has no need of prayers', he wrote in his pre-execution letter. The priest had finally to resort to a well-used strategem to give him absolution. 'Are you sorry if you've done wrong?' he asked, and Mellows answered: 'Of course I'm sorry for any wrong I've done.'

They were then taken out to the prison yard where the firing squad were inexperienced, nervous from the long wait, and presumably unhappy with their task, so that the executions were badly bungled and nine pistol shots were needed for the *coups de grace* on the four merely wounded men.

The *Irish Times* carried a note soon afterwards: 'The publication of several letters which reached us yesterday on the subject of the recent executions is prohibited by order of the Free State Government.' And the paper itself, certainly no friend to Irish republicanism, commented: 'The Free State Government has committed itself to an act of "reprisal" which eclipses in sudden and tragic severity the sternest measures of the British crown during the [1919-21] conflict.'

It was just one year since the treaty had been signed in London. On the same day 'Northern Ireland' opted out of a united Ireland. The *Irish Times* took the opportunity to urge that the Boundary Commission be dropped, as its failure was foreseen and the removal of 'this haunting embarrassment' would allow the Free State government to concentrate on law and order and reconstruction in the 26 counties.

The Irish Free State was now a dominion of the British empire, its birth saluted by the volleys of a firing squad. Thomas Johnson, the Labour leader in the Dail, protested bitterly, saying: 'I am almost forced to say that I believe you have killed the new State at its birth.'

Irish ministers offered no excuses for those judicial murders. Mulcahy expressed pride in shouldering heavy responsibilities. O'Higgins said: 'It was done deliberately and in the belief that only by that method could representative government and democratic institutions be preserved here.' President Cosgrave went further: 'a diabolical conspiracy is afoot.' Terror was being met by terror and the public must not expect civilised methods. He added: 'They were dealing with the dregs of society, people who had no regard for life or property, or all that people held dear.'

Perhaps through change of plan, or maybe through missed opportunities, the IRA killed no other Leinster House deputies in the civil war.

1923 crisis months

In the new year some peace moves were under way by outsiders and others. They included some genuine well-wishers but all were without effect on those participants who actually mattered: the Mulcahy-Cosgrave government which wanted the total defeat of their enemies, and the 'die-hard' Republicans led by Liam Lynch who believed they were fighting for freedom in an ancient tradition.

The peace movements failed to gather momentum even after a dreadful incident when one Leinster House deputy's home was set on fire by an IRA active service unit and his seven-year-old child was burned to death by accident.

In 1923, from January to March, the Republican forces were losing the war, and yet most of them refused to consider surrender or even a compromise despite increasing hardships, lack of supplies, dwindling numbers, the loss of much popular support, and the sufferings of themselves and their supporters.

During those winter months the official executions continued relentlessly, and the unofficial ones, too. IRA men were secretly court-martialled and shot, usually in groups of three or four throughout the 26 counties, so that it seemed that the Free State's military command wished that personal responsibility should be spread amongst its senior officers. There were 77 official court-martial executions. Sentences were passed against prisoners who were denied the rank of soldiers and all the relevant documents were later destroyed. Usually IRA volunteers would be tried by regular courts-martial and shot next dawn without publicity, but up in Donegal four IRA officers were shot in Drumboe Castle after a night's drumhead session, after months of imprisonment there.

Throughout this period the Republicans saw how the Free Staters annexed to themselves all the outward trappings of the Republic: the tricolour flag, the claim to the 1916-1921 tradition, even the name of Dail Eireann for their Leinster House parliament, together with the claim that Pearse and Connolly would have backed their 26-counties state. Meanwhile the Staters executed, imprisoned, deprived and threatened those who carried on the fight of Connolly and Pearse.

It was during that dark period that a bitter little song was written, compressing Republican feelings into simple but passionate lines. The words are still heard in Ireland, although often altered and updated.

Take it down from the mast, Irish traitors,
The flag we Republicans claim.
It can never belong to Free Staters,
You've brought on it nothing but shame.

You've murdered brave Liam and Rory,
You've taken young Richard and Joe.
Your hands with their blood are all gory,
Fulfilling the work of the foe.

But we stand with Enright and Larkin,
With Daly and Sullivan bold.
We'll break down the English connection
And bring back the nation you sold.

So leave it to those who are willing
To uphold it in war or in peace:
The ones who intend to defend it
Until England's tyranny cease.

County Kerry atrocities

Through all the violence and destruction of the civil war, one episode stands out as particularly horrible. It was perpetrated by the Free State military and condoned by their government.

During the civil war the county of Kerry was a Republican stronghold and so it took time for the Staters to crush its resistance. A special Dublin Guards taskforce was sent there as soon as possible under the command of Brigadier-General Daly. 'No one told me to bring kid gloves, so I didn't', Daly said afterwards, and systematic brutalities were practised in Kerry more often than elsewhere.

In March 1923 a Free State officer, accused of habitually torturing prisoners, was killed by a trigger-mine ambush on a lonely road. The next day nine IRA prisoners, one with a broken arm, another with a fractured wrist, and one crippled by spinal injuries after their torture in the local barracks, were brought by lorry to a country wood near Ballyseedy. There they were bound with ropes and roped together around a land-mine which the Staters had prepared and which they then exploded. Bits of bodies were scattered far and wide. Pieces of flesh were left hanging on the trees. But by a freak blast one man was blown clear and unharmed into a ditch and managed to escape unseen, his clothes scorched off him, with a severed hand tied against his wrist.

On the same day, in a different area, four other IRA prisoners were deliberately torn to shreds by a mine and by bombs then hurled at them, but once again another man was thrown clear and ran to safety across the fields. What remained of the rest was put into coffins and a false report was given out that the 'Irregulars' had been killed while working on their own mines.

A few days later, outside Cahirciveen, five more IRA men (also tortured) were killed by the Staters with a mine used in the same way, but on that occasion all five had first been shot in the legs to prevent any more miraculous escapes. A Free State officer resigned in protest over what he had witnessed and later publicised the true account.

A subsequent low-key inquiry whitewashed all concerned. The Free State's immediate response was a military order that all Kerry prisoners 'who die whilst in military custody' must be buried by troops at the place of execution. This was to avoid repetition of the violent scenes when families opened the coffins at the funerals and saw the contents. And the Catholic bishops, so vocal on some matters, remained strangely silent about what the crows ate in Kerry.

Ceasefire

By April 1923 the Republican army was still operational but few of its original leaders were still alive and free. The round-ups were daily more effective and the health and morale of many were badly affected after a winter of being hunted through poor and rough country.

The Free State army numbered some 60,000 men, properly equipped and fed and paid. An IRA brigade might number less than 20 men, with a few rifles shared between them and their supply dumps constantly raided. Almost the final blow came when their Chief of Staff, Liam Lynch, who had continued certain of ultimate victory, was fatally wounded during a routine round-up in the Knockmealdown mountains while on his way to an IRA Executive meeting where he would have opposed any talk of giving up. He was shot from a distance by a Free State soldier and died later that day in hospital on 10 April 1923.

A remnant of the IRA's Executive managed to meet and unanimously agreed that although the independence of the Irish nation and the integrity of its territory were inalienable, they would consent that the Sinn Fein president, Eamon de Valera, should seek peace terms with the Free State government.

The decision was reached for military reasons because they knew that their weary, sick and scattered units were hardly capable of sustaining another summer campaign, and not through pressure by peace movements or loss of personal convictions. Those leaders that were left wished to preserve the Republican cause by finding some acceptable means to stop the fighting. However, Free State president Cosgrave would not negotiate, nor would he discuss any alternative proposals with intermediaries. This rigid refusal and vindictive attitude ensured that there would not be a genuine peace settlement.

Therefore, in order to bring the war to an end by the best means they could, both the IRA command and de Valera's underground government issued statements to the Irish people, neither admitting complete defeat nor pretending the present struggle could continue.

Frank Aiken, the new Chief of Staff, ordered all units of the Irish Republican Army to observe a ceasefire from noon, Monday 30 April. One month later this was followed by a final order for the dumping of arms, in order to hide weapons and ammunition ready for another day: 'the arms with which we have fought the enemies of our country are to be dumped. The foreign and domestic enemies of the Republic have for the moment prevailed.'

Although the war came to an end in May 1923, there was not much difference between war and peace for Republicans, who were still being arrested, imprisoned and even murdered in the months to come.

The 10 months of war had been worse than the three years of war against the British in terms of lives lost, ruin of property which included the great Anglo-Irish houses and valuable estates, damage to the economy, and an enduring apparatus of state repression. £30,000,000 was a most conservative estimate of the cost in financial terms, a disastrous sum by the money values of the time for the already impoverished 26 counties.

The war emphasised the national divide between those Irish who instinctively turn towards Britain and those who instinctively do not.

The August 1923 election and aftermath

With the country outwardly pacified, the Free State government judged it a good time to call another general election to confirm themselves in office. They stood under the new name of Cumann na nGaedhael (later to become part of Fine Gael), but they misjudged the mood of the people. They also made the mistake of allowing political Republicans to take part under the old banner of Sinn Fein. The voters had not forgotten the attractions of that name.

As in the August 1923 general election, Republican women had a vital role in the hunger strike campaign that soon followed.

The government had the usual support of the press and strong backing from the earlier pro-treaty elements. Sinn Fein suffered continual harassment and disruption, with most of its candidates interned or on the run. (As a result, women and youth played the major part in electioneering.) In view of its apparent advantages, the result came as an unpleasant shock for the government. They had won the largest number of seats, 63, but Sinn Fein had won 44 – more than twice their best hopes. It greatly boosted Republican morale after all their misfortunes since the treaty. The remaining seats were shared between Labour, Farmers and Independents.

There had been signs during the campaign that the Free State government was not having it all its own way. Reports told how William Cosgrave raged over his reception in what was supposed to be a friendly area — being unable to hire the local bands, an unwelcome guest at a hurling match, and then finding a memorial card for Liam Mellows and Erskine Childers under his plate at an official dinner. And of how in County Kerry black-shawled mothers knelt in the streets and cursed him for the murder of their sons. It appeared that sufficient voters had drawn

Sinn Fein election headquarters in 1923.

on a reservoir of sympathy for ill-treated Republicans, while also wanting to record their resentment at the harsh measures and visible arrogance of the government.

The war had left the country in poor shape. At last the Free State government could concentrate on making its new Ireland, much in the same mould as the old one, with the British connection as firmly cemented as ever James Connolly had warned it would be if the green flag was merely hoisted above Dublin Castle without setting about the organisation of the socialist Republic.

The British crown's Lord Lieutenant in Dublin became titled the king's Governor-General and presided over a slightly different layer of Irish society. Amongst those who did not attend top-hatted garden parties at Viceregal Lodge were the 13,000 prisoners crammed into jails and camps. And since Kevin O'Higgins, Minister for Home Affairs, had promised caustically that 'This is not going to be a draw, with a replay in the autumn', there they were going to stay. During the 1923 summer further measures were put through parliament, including the Public Safety (Emergency Powers) (No.2) Act 1923, by which Richard Mulcahy as Minister for Defence signed individual orders for the further detention of men and women already interned without trial.

As a result of the election, in terms of elected representatives, the Free State government was left in a minority position with only 63 seats out of a total of 153. This was transformed into a clear majority by the simple expedient of banning Sinn Fein members when they still refused to take the oath of allegiance to the British king and thereby accept the treaty. Moreover, 18 of the Sinn Fein elected TDs were prisoners. In an enduring Irish tradition they had been elected even while in jail, but would not be released to take their seats. One of the 18 was de Valera who had come out of hiding to address a public meeting in his County Clare constituency of Ennis. Free State troops fired at the platform, wounding people, and de Valera was arrested.

So when the new parliament assembled, all Sinn Fein TDs were absent and the Cosgrave party remained firmly in power. 'Those who talk about democracy cannot say, I think, that democracy in the 1923 election got very much of a chance,' de Valera remarked bitterly from his cell.

The prisoners

For the many thousands of Republican prisoners the summer and autumn of 1923 was a desperate time. And because one legacy of the

Irish civil war for all future Dublin governments would be numbers of IRA prisoners, the subject requires some attention when studying the implications of that war. The prisoners were kept in appalling conditions in jails, internment camps, cellars of court-houses, army barracks, workhouses and a prison ship. Already the prisoners in Maryborough (now called Portlaoise) had tried to burn down their prison.

Their situation was made worse by a political decision taken at Free State cabinet level to criminalise them. The implementation of this policy began in earnest in September 1923 with the appointment of a new military governor to Dublin's Mountjoy prison, whose aim was to turn Republican prisoners into 'ordinary criminals' in the eyes of the general public. Until then, all those held in the jails as well as the camps had been living in a similar way to those special category men in the Long Kesh 'cages' who even today effectively retain a POW status.

There was fierce resistance within Mountjoy and a new war developed between the IRA and their armed guards. Ernie O'Malley later wrote a detailed account of imprisonment in which he described the attitudes of his companions, who showed the same defiant spirit that Irish Republican prisoners everywhere seem able to sustain:

Exercise was restricted; sanitation and the cleanliness of the wing was interfered with, and gradually the attempt to ignore our prison organisation under our own officers increased in intensity. It looked as if the attempt meant the beginning of a plan to treat us as criminals.

Further restrictions were imposed, and the attempt continued to break down resistance and methodically deprive us of our privileges, so that eventually our captors could impose criminal status by degrees, and use its acceptance as an excuse to apply it to newly arrested prisoners. They had not learned the lesson that the British had, when numbers of our men were in prison.

Free men cannot be kept in jail, for their spirits are free, and jail for political prisoners is always a duel; we were not prisoners of war, no prisoner had been conceded political rights, and the duel went on. Positions are usually reversed, for jailers and warders have to peep and pry, to be ever on the alert, to glue their eyes to keyholes, to listen at cell doors, and to deal with what to them is an unknown quantity – the spirit of freedom.

In our code it is the duty of prisoners to prove that they cannot be influenced by their surroundings, or affected by the personalities of jailers. A prisoner must reverse their whole system, place them in the position of prisoners, make them concentrate on petty doings and sayings, limit their minds to the confines of prison walls. Make the enemy feel a jailer but be free himself. Prisoners have to maintain a constant fight to prevent being dominated by their surroundings. Individual as well as co-ordinated action is always necessary to enable

RELEASE THE PRISONERS !

There are 13,000 Prisoners in Goal : ROTTING.

You know what they are suffering. If you don't ask their relatives.

Many of their relatives are literally : STARVING.

There are in Kilmaniham Gaol alone 500 Girls. HOW MANY DID ENGLAND PUT IN GAOL ?

Hunger-strike after hunger-strike had taken place in these bastilles in an attempt by the prisoners to lessen the sufferings of those among them whom they know to be unable to bear their privations.

KNOW THE TRUTH despite the Censor's gag of the past twelve months.

These men have suffered in the gaols of TWO "governments."

HAVE YOU NO GRATITUDE ?

Release the Prisoners.

The Republican publicity department did its best to mobilise support for the prisoners.

men to realize that only by such organization can they realize their strength and effectively nullify or destroy a prison system.

Following a serious riot in Mountjoy, in which hundreds took part, the prisoners resorted to a mass hunger strike in order to obtain their unconditional release. To strike for political status or better treatment was thought an insufficient reason since the war had been over for many months. On 13 October 1923 the prisoners' OC smuggled out a manifesto from Mountjoy which announced the virtually unanimous decision:

> In face of all these facts, the prisoners now feel that there is but one alternative left to them – the hunger strike, the ultimate weapon of passive resistance, and that they have decided to adopt...
>
> Each of us to himself and to his comrades solemnly pledges himself to abstain from food until he is unconditionally released. In taking this grave decision we, as citizens of Ireland, know that lovers of liberty the world over will understand and respect our motives.
>
> Our lives and the sufferings we shall endure we offer to God for the furtherance of the course of truth and justice in every land and for the speeding of the day of Ireland's freedom.

The government refused to give way and so the hunger strike followed a familiar course. The newspapers gave little or no coverage until the final stages. Cabinet ministers stood firm against what they

Two women in the forefront of the street marches and demonstrations during the 1923 hunger strike were Charlotte Despard and Maud Gonne MacBride, carrying the placard.

condemned as criminal blackmail. The public conscience was generally unmoved, although numbers of individuals and organisations did show deep concern, and meantime the prisoners suffered. No one had been ordered to go on hunger strike or to remain on it. It was always a personal choice, although obviously prisoners felt a sense of duty to their comrades. The IRA and Sinn Fein outside neither ordered the hunger strike nor greatly approved of it, but once it started they gave all possible support.

The hunger strike began in Mountjoy with about 400 men involved but quickly spread to the other camps and jails who went on strike in solidarity, including the women's prison, until at one time an estimated 8,000 prisoners were refusing to take food. This vast number practically ensured the strike's collapse because few can endure a prolonged hunger strike. When thousands broke the strike in the early stages and began to eat again, the government was able to make good propaganda out of it.

The original leaders were removed from Mountjoy to Kilmainham jail where most of them continued until the ending of the strike on 23 November, after 41 days and after two had died. The body of one of the dead hunger-strikers was refused admission to a Cork church by order of the bishop.

The strike was brought to an end without any concessions whatsoever being granted, and grievous harm had been done to health. But the government then began to release large numbers of men and women over the Christmas period and in the new year, so that those prisoners who remained were consoled by the belief that they had won a moral victory.

Afterwards

By the summer of 1924, most of the Republican prisoners had been released, into a society in which most avenues of employment were closed to them. Thousands of Republican activists emigrated in the years immediately following the civil war.

In 1924, Richard Mulcahy resigned from government and military office over a Free State army dispute. He remained a Leinster House TD but never regained power. In the same year de Valera was released and moved towards 'slightly constitutional' politics. Three years later Kevin O'Higgins, Cosgrave's heir-apparent, was assassinated while on his way to church and those who killed him were never apprehended.

In 1925, the Boundary Commission, promised by the treaty,

FOR two years the people of Republican Spain have fought against the combined forces of Mussolini and Hitler.

Barcelona, Madrid, Bilbao, Tortosa and other centres in Spain, have suffered the horrors of air raids. Mussolini openly boasts that he is sending the airplanes, bombs and pilots responsible for the cruel warfare against the women and children of Republican Spain.

This is supposed to be a civil war. It is nothing of the kind. The Spanish people are fighting for liberty against a foreign Fascist invasion.

Frank Ryan, Republican fighter and leader of the Irish Unit, International Brigade, is now a prisoner in a Franco jail. Italian officers control Franco territory and it is they who hold Frank Ryan prisoner. DEMAND HIS RELEASE!

The people of Dublin can extend no welcome to the warships of Mussolini -- the user of poison gas, the betrayer of Austria, the bomber of Spanish women and children and the jailer of Frank Ryan.

inevitably found in favour of Britain and Northern Ireland. The border was to remain as it was and there would be no overall Council of Ireland. Cosgrave's unfortunate public comment was that it was 'a damn good bargain'. In private he admitted, 'We were codded.' To the Irish Labour Party it was 'an unmitigated betrayal'. Sir James Craig at Stormont was triumphant.

Some thirteen years after the civil war ended, some of the protagonists faced each other again, but on a battlefield far away from Ireland. This time the civil war was in Spain, and among Franco's supporters was the Army Comrades Association, known as the 'Blueshirts', which had been started by former Free State Army officers.

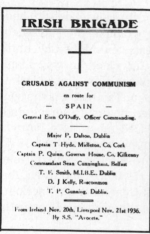

IRISH BRIGADE

✝

CRUSADE AGAINST COMMUNISM

en route for

— SPAIN —

General Eoin O'Duffy, Officer Commanding.

Major P. Dalton, Dublin
Captain T Hyde, Midleton, Co. Cork
Captain P. Quinn, Gowran House, Co. Kilkenny
Commandant Sean Cunningham, Belfast
T. F. Smith, M.I.B.E., Dublin
D. J Kelly, Roscommon
T. P. Gunning, Dublin.

From Ireland Nov. 20th, Liverpool Nov. 21st 1936.
By S.S. "Avoceta."

This page: the Blueshirts were Irish fascists who supported Franco in the Spanish civil war. Their leader Eoin O'Duffy was a former Free State army general and police chief.

Left: Frank Ryan became commander of the Irish in the International Brigades. Ryan had fought with the IRA in the Irish civil war, had been arrested many times for his republican activities, and was a former editor of An Phoblacht. *The poster was produced to protest against a visit of Mussolini's navy to Dublin.*

Many republicans and radicals, including some who had fought for the Irish Republic in 1922-1923, also went to Spain. They joined the International Brigade to fight for the Spanish Republic. While the Blueshirts received the blessing of the Irish Catholic bishops, the supporters of the Spanish Republic were frequently harassed by the Free State authorities.

Political legacies

The course of the current propaganda war, and the nature of political parties in the 26 counties, should be seen in the historical context of the civil war years. Otherwise much from Dublin would be incomprehensible, as for instance its long-lasting co-operation with Westminster over the six north-eastern counties and its reactionary attitudes towards the national struggle. The explanation is in the repressive history of Fine Gael, the acquiescence of Labour, and the ambivalence of Fianna Fail.

Fine Gael

Many of the current Fine Gael deputies in Leinster House are kith and kin of those who ruled during the civil war. For example, the Taoiseach (Prime Minister) during the mid 1970s, and the leader of Fine Gael until his enforced resignation after losing the 1977 election, was Liam Cosgrave, son of President William Cosgrave of the Free State. Garret FitzGerald, the party's next leader and the present Taoiseach, is the son of Desmond FitzGerald, a cabinet minister under the first Cosgrave, and the first to agree to the judicial murders of 8 December 1922. Patrick Cooney, Minister for Justice until his personal defeat at the polls in 1977 (a handful of privileged voters then sent him to the Irish Senate from which he emerged to be first Minister for Defence and then for Education), is the nephew of the Free State's General Sean MacEoin, whose name appeared on IRA death lists because they charged him with the murder and torturing of prisoners.

Labour Party

James Connolly's eldest daughter, Nora, denounced the shame of her father's party in joining in coalitions with the Fine Gael political descendants of the civil war Staters. She also said that she regretted accepting de Valera's offer to enter the Leinster House Senate.

It is hard to find socialists amongst the Leinster House Labour group. They appear to be either social democrats or else of the ilk of their former minister, Dr. Conor Cruise O'Brien, who is still probably the best-known Irish example of a West Briton.

Fianna Fail

De Valera wished to enter Leinster House politics and when his proposals were rejected by a majority of Sinn Fein delegates at a special conference in 1926, he resigned and founded his own party, Fianna Fail. That party won 44 seats in the June 1927 general election, only three seats less than Fine Gael. Soon afterwards they signed the oath of allegiance to the British Crown – then a prequisite of entering the Leinster House parliament – and took their seats, becoming the main opposition party.

In 1932 Fianna Fail took office for the first time. The IRA had helped Fianna Fail's campaign in order to defeat Cosgrave. Sinn Fein retained its abstentionist position and stood aside. When the IRA continued its war against Britain and British interests, the de Valera government turned on them as harshly as would ever Fine Gael. The Irish Republican Army was declared an illegal organisation, and new legislation allowed for military tribunals, internment, heavy jail sentences, and the death penalty for 'treason' and other offences. The pattern had been set.

When out of power, Fianna Fail has a habit of getting back into office by making republican noises, usually through calls for a British withdrawal from the north, and by posing as defenders of the workers and small farmers. When in office it has a habit of using the same old emergency powers together with some new ones of its own. And yet because of its Sinn Fein antecedents a certain separatist sentiment remains. Fianna Fail leaders give lip service to republican ideals, while continuing as the practised pragmatists of Dublin politics.

Progressive Democrats

A recent product of troubled 26 county politics is the Progressive Democrats, a hybrid party which has picked up disgruntled members from Fianna Fail and Fine Gael alike. It originated from a piqued Fianna Fail clique and then assimilated many ex-Fine Gael supporters who fitted well into its general image of right-wing middle class.

Another agreement, another failure

The December 1921 treaty that was signed under duress by five unauthorised Irish delegates had been an historic pact. At the time, the British diplomatists allowed the Irish to present it as a 'treaty' and thereby make it easier to sell back home. An actual treaty could not be made except between two sovereign nations. As Ireland at that date was constitutionally a part of the United Kingdom, the correct terminology for what was in fact an early form of neo-colonialism was 'Articles of

Agreement'. That 1921 deception worked out very well for the British government.

Some 64 years later, another Anglo-Irish agreement propped up the British in Ireland. The Hillsborough deal of November 1985 was designed to protect British interests in Ireland and once again an Irish government accepted the wrong end of a bargain. The Hillsborough deal made no attempt to reunify the country; instead, the obvious intention was to block further Republican successes, whether military or political. It aimed to gain increased collaboration from Dublin against Republicans, and to get more co-operation in running the six counties from the Social Democratic and Labour Party, which represents the interests of the nationalist middle class there.

The new agreement will not bring any real improvements for the oppressed nationalist community in the north. Rather, like the treaty of 1921, it delays the day when peace will be achieved. This can only come about through the ending of British rule in the north, the ending of partition, and the emergence of a truly independent Ireland.

Right: The official welcome across the border — and the unofficial warnings. In 1968 the current phase of the northern struggle was getting under way.

OUR FIGHT
IS FOR
THE BASIC
HUMAN RIGHTS

FULL
= CIVIL RIGHTS
NOW

WELCOME
TO
NORTHERN
IRELAND

Co. ARMAGH

B. SPECIALS
ORANGE
MILITIA!

SPECIAL
LAWS
FOR
SPECIAL POLICE

Liam Mellows at Bodenstown outside Dublin just before the start of the civil war. He gave the annual oration to honour Wolfe Tone, one of the eighteenth century founders of Irish republicanism.

Further reading

Sean Cronin, *Irish Nationalism*, Dublin: Academy Press 1980, London: Pluto Press 1983.

Sean Cronin, *The McGarrity Papers*, Dublin: Anvil Books 1972.

C. Desmond Greaves, *Liam Mellows and the Irish Revolution*, London: Lawrence and Wishart 1971.

Kenneth Griffith and Timothy O'Grady, *Curious Journey*, London: Hutchinson 1982.

Dorothy Macardle, *The Irish Republic*, Gollancz 1937, London: Corgi 1968.

Dorothy Macardle, *Tragedies of Kerry*, Dublin: Elo Press 1924.

Uinseann MacEoin, *Survivors*, Dublin: Argenta Publications 1980.

Walter Macken, *The Scorching Wind*, London: Pan Books 1966 (fiction).

David Martin, *The Road to Ballyshannon*, London: Abacus 1983 (fiction).

Eoin Neeson, *The Civil War in Ireland*, Cork: Mercier Press 1969.

Sean O'Casey, *Inishfaallen, Fare Thee Well*, London: Pan Books 1972.

Frank O'Connor, *An Only Child*, London: Pan Books 1970.

Peadar O'Donnell, *The Gates Flew Open*, Cork: Mercier Press 1966.

Florence O'Donoghue, *No Other Law*, Dublin: Irish Press 1954.

Ernie O'Malley, *The Singing Flame*, Dublin: Anvil Books 1978.

Margaret Ward, *Unmanageable Revolutionaries*, London: Pluto Press 1983.

Calton Younger, *Ireland's Civil War*, London: Fontana 1979.

Two important primary sources, giving opposing viewpoints on the civil war, are available in the National Library in Dublin. These are the papers of J.J. 'Ginger' O'Connell, on the Free State side, and those of J.J. O'Donovan on the Republican side.

A film on the treaty negotiations

Breakdown is a new 24-minute colour film, available on video, by Gerry Floyd. The film is set against a backdrop of Ireland's war of independence from 1920-1922. It centres on a dramatic reconstruction of the peace negotiations between the British and Irish governments which led to the signing of the Anglo-Irish treaty in December 1921. Actors play key figures, including Michael Collins, Arthur Griffith and Lloyd George; songs and documentary film are also used. This was a crucial period in Irish history, and the effects of many of the decisions made then are still being felt in Ireland today.

Breakdown is available for sale or hire on VHS video from The Other Cinema, 79 Wardour Street, London W1V 3TH, tel. 01-734 8508/9.

Back cover photograph: Republicans patrolling Grafton Street in Dublin in June 1922 shortly before the attack on the Four Courts.